The Creepy-Crawly Book

65p

For other titles in the Target Series see end pages

The
Creepy-Crawly
Book

Legends, stories and poems about fearful creatures

Edited by LUCY BERMAN

a division of
Universal-Tandem Publishing Co., Ltd.,
14 Gloucester Road, London SW7 4RD

First published simultaneously in Great Britain

by Allan Wingate (Publishers) Ltd.,
and Universal-Tandem Publishing Co., Ltd., 1973

ISBN 0 426 10241 X

Printed in Great Britain by litho by The Anchor Press Ltd., and
bound by Wm. Brendon & Son Ltd., both of Tiptree, Essex

Dedication:

To the pupils of the Central Foundation Schools in Islington, North London, without whose help this anthology could not have been compiled.

Acknowledgements

The Editor is grateful to the following authors, agents and publishers for permission to include copyright material in this anthology: The Executors of the Estate of H. G. Wells for 'The Valley of the Spiders'; the author, Dennis Dobson, Ltd., for 'Good Company' by Leonard Clark; Mrs George Bambridge, MacMillan & Co., of Basingstoke and London, and MacMillan & Co., of Canada for 'Rikki-Tikki-Tavi'; Popular Science for 'Old Rattler and the King Snake' by David Starr Jordan; the author, J. M. Dent and Sons, for 'The Cobra', 'The Ant', and 'The Termite' from 'The Face is Familiar' by Ogden Nash; Harcourt Brace Jovanovich, Inc., for 'Worms and the Wind' from 'Complete Poems' by Carl Sandburg; the author, Curtis Brown, Ltd., for 'The Curse of Mouse Tower' from 'Haunted Houses' by Bernhardt J. Hurwood; the author, A.M. Heath & Co., for 'The Mouse' by Henry Williamson, and MacDonald & Jane's, Ltd., for the accompanying illustration; Meredith Corporation an extract from 'Edge of the Jungle' by William Beebe; Miss Joan M. Beadon for 'Rats'; Associated Book Publishers, Ltd., for 'Bats' from 'The Lost World' by Randall Jarrell; Richard Henwood for 'The Scorpion'; the author, Granada Publishing, Ltd., for 'Wilhelmina' and accompanying illustration from 'Encounters with Animals' by Gerald Durrell; and Dodd, Mead & Co., for an extract from 'The Ant People' by Hans Heinz Ewers.

Contents

Editor's Foreword

IV—SCORPIONS AND ANTS

V—HORRORS OF THE DEEP

Illustrations

Introduction

What living thing would you *least* like to be left alone with in a room late at night? A squat-bodied creature with eight, long, hairy legs? A smooth, slippery, limbless creature? Perhaps a fierce, bright-eyed creature with razor-sharp teeth and a thin, naked tail? The spider, the snake, the rat and other creepy-crawly beasts are the basis of many people's nightmares. Many otherwise brave individuals of both sexes would try any means of escape from a room that contained a snake, for example, whether or not it was poisonous or at all harmful.

There are people who say that man has an instinctive fear of snakes, and that it is 'natural' to fear them. This fear, however, is not universal. Some people enjoy watching snakes, handling them, observing them—even keeping them as pets. They say that one's attitude to snakes arises from early teaching; that a child who screams at the sight of a snake is likely to have a parent who feels faint at the sight of a worm.

Fear of a certain creature sometimes seems to be prompted by the way in which the creature moves. The silent slither of a snake often inspires horror; so does the apparently aimless fluttering of a bat or a moth. The sudden movement of rats is something that I myself find quite horrible, although I am not much affected by it except at night, in deserted places.

The idea for this book came from the responses of pupils in two North London schools to the question which opened this foreword: 'What living thing would you *least* like to be left alone with in a room late at night?' Their first four choices, namely spiders, snakes, rats and mice, and ants, indicated that it is the humbler 'creepy-crawlies' that people are most frightened of. So it was decided to make a creepy-crawly book, exploring the way that these feared and despised creatures have been regarded in mythology and literature.

This is a book of many moods. There are moments—especially in H. G. Wells' 'The Valley of Spiders'—of sheer, nightmarish horror, and others which will send cold chills down the reader's spine. But it would be unfair, in fact libellous, to deal only with the horrific side of these creatures. As I mentioned before, there are people who like snakes, and others, like Granfer Jearge in Henry Williamson's story, who became greatly attached to pet mice and rats. It is necessary to be objective, as William Beebe was in relation to vampire bats, and sometimes scientific objectivity prompts affection, as Gerald Durrell found when he began looking after the whip-scorpion, Wilhelmina.

By the time you have finished this book, it is hoped that you will have had a few fresh thoughts about creepy-crawlies, and perhaps you will look with new eyes at that spider crawling up the wall—and then again, you may be moving too fast to do very much thinking about it.

LUCY BERMAN

Spiders

The Legend of Arachne

Lucy Berman

The ancient Greeks told an unusual story to account for the origin of spiders. They said that in the days before spiders, there was a girl named Arachne, who loved to spin and weave. She came from a village called Colophon, which was famous for its purple dye. Many good weavers worked in Colophon, but none was as skilful as she.

All day, and every day, Arachne sat at her loom, weaving a web of delicate wool. The long threads of the warp hung down from a beam overhead, and Arachne, quick-fingered, passed the shuttle through these threads, drawing a strand of yarn from side to side. Again and again she did this, stopping after each throw of the shuttle to press the new strand firmly upwards. As she worked, a picture emerged. Flowers bloomed on the web, a river ran across it, a bird sat open-mouthed in silent song.

As long as there was light, Arachne wove. Her family were proud of her remarkable talent. Strangers to Colophon heard about Arachne before they were told anything else. So quickly did she work and so deftly, that people came to watch her at her loom.

In time, Arachne grew conceited. Knowing that her

tapestries were always the best, she decided that she was obviously superior to everyone around her. This angered her sisters and worried her parents. Arachne was so single-minded, too absorbed in her work: it wasn't natural, her parents thought. And when would she marry—a girl so proud that she would not even speak to most people?

One day, as Arachne was weaving away surrounded by admirers, an old woman came and stood near her. She was a stranger to the village, a decrepit old hag, bent and shrunken by extreme age. Her bright eyes followed every movement of the girl's swift fingers, and she nodded in approval.

'Excellent work, my daughter,' she said in a harsh, high voice.

Arachne ignored her.

The old woman put her head to one side and stared thoughtfully. 'I suppose you pray to the goddess Athene, to thank her for this gift of weaving?'

Arachne raised her eyes and answered proudly. 'My skill is my own. Athene did not teach me. I dare say, if she were here, we should soon see who was the better weaver.'

Many of the villagers were shocked by this answer, but the old hag laughed. 'She is here!' she cried exultantly. As she spoke, the years fell from her back and she stood before them tall, straight and gleaming: the goddess Athene!

Arachne turned pale. She was frightened and angry. 'How unfair,' she thought, 'to play such tricks. But it does not matter. I am as good a weaver as anyone.'

Aloud, she said to Athene, 'Here are two looms ready for weaving, And here is thread of many colours.'

The goddess sat at one loom, Arachne at the other. They wove at an equal pace, so quickly that the vil-

16

lagers gasped to see their fingers fly. Arachne, in her anger, wove a tapestry filled with scenes showing the deceitfulness of the gods. She depicted gods in disguise, taking advantage of mortal men. So beautiful was her work that the figures seemed alive, as if they could move or speak.

When both weavers had finished, Arachne looked with satisfaction at her own work. Calmly she turned to see Athene's tapestry. The goddess had created scenes of her own triumphs, and her work was so inspired that her woven image seemed as real as her living presence. Where Arachne's figures looked as if they should be capable of speech, Athene's seemed still more vivid, convincing the villagers that they actually heard voices coming from the loom.

Arachne was defeated and overcome with shame. Leaving her loom, she went to a lonely olive tree, and hung herself from its branches.

Athene, following, saw that Arachne's pride was now all gone. Not wishing her to suffer death, she touched Arachne with her finger, saying, 'You shall spin your webs, my daughter. You and yours, the spiders, the *Arachnidae*, shall spin from now until eternity.'

Arachne changed into a spider and the rope from which she hung became a thread. She climbed up the thread on her slender legs and at once began spinning a delicate web—absorbed, as always, in her work.

The Legend of Robert the Bruce and the Spider

Sir Walter Scott

The King met with many sad encounters amidst his
dangerous and dismal wanderings; yet, though almost
always defeated by numbers of the English, and of such
Scots as sided with them, he still kept up his own spirits
and those of his followers. He was a better scholar than
was usual in those days, when, except clergymen, few
people learned to read and write. But King Robert
could do both very well; and we are told that he sometimes read aloud to his companions to amuse them,
when they were crossing the great Highland lakes in such
wretched leaky boats as they could find for the purpose.

At last dangers increased so much around the brave
King Robert, that he was obliged to separate himself
from the ladies and his Queen; for the winter was coming on, and it would be impossible for the women to
endure this wandering sort of life when the frost and
snow should arrive. So he left his queen, with the
Countess of Buchan and others, in the only castle which
remained to him, which was called Kildrummie, and
is situated near the head of the river Don in Aberdeen-
shire. The King also left his youngest brother, Nigel
Bruce, to defend the castle against the English; and he
himself, with his second brother Edward, who was a

very brave man, but still more rash and passionate than Robert himself, went over to an island called Rachrin, off the coast of Ireland, where Bruce and the few men that followed his fortunes passed the winter of 1306.

In the meantime, ill luck seemed to pursue all his friends in Scotland. The Castle of Kildrummie was taken by the English, and Nigel Bruce, a beautiful and brave youth, was cruelly put to death by the victors. The ladies who had attended on Robert's queen, as well as the queen herself, and the Countess of Buchan, were thrown into strict confinement, and treated with the utmost severity. This news reached Bruce while he was residing in a miserable dwelling at Rachrin, and reduced him to the point of despair.

It was about this time than an incident took place, which, although it rests only on tradition in families of the name of Bruce, is rendered probable by the manners of the times. After receiving the last unpleasing intelligence from Scotland, Bruce was lying one morning on his wretched bed, and deliberating with himself whether he had not better resign all thoughts of again attempting to make good his right to the Scottish crown, and, dismissing his followers, transport himself and his brothers to the Holy Land, and spend the rest of his life in fighting against the Saracens; by which he thought, perhaps, he might deserve the forgiveness of Heaven for the great sin of stabbing Comyn in the church at Dumfries. But then, on the other hand, he thought it would be both criminal and cowardly to give up his attempts to restore freedom to Scotland, while there yet remained the least chance of his being successful in an undertaking which, rightly considered, was much more his duty than to drive the infidels out of Palestine, though the superstition of his age might think otherwise.

While he was divided betwixt these reflections, and

doubtful of what he should do, Bruce was looking upward to the roof of the cabin in which he lay; and his eye was attracted by a spider, which, hanging at the end of a long thread of its own spinning, was endeavouring, as is the fashion of that creature, to swing itself from one beam in the roof to another, for the purpose of fixing the line on which it meant to stretch its web. The insect made the attempt again and again without success; and at length Bruce counted that it had tried to carry its point six times, and been as often unable to do so. It came into his head that he had himself fought just six battles against the English and their allies, and that the poor persevering spider was exactly in the same situation with himself, having made as many trials, and been as often disappointed in what it aimed at. 'Now,' thought Bruce, 'as I have no means of knowing what is best to be done, I will be guided by the luck which shall attend this spider. If the insect shall make another effort to fix its thread, and shall be successful, I will venture a seventh time to try my fortune in Scotland; but if the spider shall fail, I will go to the wars in Palestine, and never return to my native country more.'

While Bruce was forming this resolution, the spider made another exertion with all the force it could muster, and fairly succeeded in fastening its thread to the beam which it had so often in vain attempted to reach. Bruce, seeing the success of the spider, resolved to try his own fortune; and as he had never before gained a victory, so he never afterwards sustained any considerable or decisive check or defeat. I have often met with people of the name of Bruce, so completely persuaded of the truth of this story that they would not on any account kill a spider; because it was that insect which had shown the example of perseverance, and given a signal of good luck to their great namesake.

The Valley of the Spiders

H. G. Wells

Towards midday the three pursuers came abruptly round a bend in the torrent bed upon the sight of a very broad and spacious valley. The difficult and winding trench of pebbles along which they had tracked the fugitives for so long, expanded to a broad slope, and with a common impulse the three men left the trail, and rode to a low eminence set with olive-dun trees, and there halted, the two others, as became them, a little behind the man with the silver-studded bridle.

For a space they scanned the great expanse below them with eager eyes. It spread remoter and remoter, with only a few clusters of sere thorn bushes here and there, and the dim suggestions of some now waterless ravine to break its desolation of yellow grass. Its purple distances melted at last into the bluish slopes of the further hills—hills it might be of a greener kind—and above them invisibly supported, and seeming indeed to hang in the blue, were the snow-clad summits of mountains—that grew larger and bolder to the north-westward as the sides of the valley drew together. And westward the valley opened until a distant darkness under the sky told where the forest began. But the three men looked neither east nor west, but only steadfastly across the valley.

The gaunt man with the scarred lip was the first to speak. 'Nowhere,' he said, with a sigh of disappointment in his voice. 'But after all, they had a full day's start.'

'They don't know we are after them,' said the little man on the white horse.

'*She* would know,' said the leader bitterly, as if speaking to himself.

'Even then they can't go fast. They've got no beast but the mule, and all today the girl's foot has been bleeding——'

The man with the silver bridle flashed a quick intensity of rage on him. 'Do you think I haven't seen that?' he snarled.

'It helps, anyhow,' whispered the little man to himself.

The gaunt man with the scarred lip stared impassively. 'They can't be over the valley,' he said. 'If we ride hard——'

He glanced at the white horse and paused.

'Curse all white horses!' said the man with the silver bridle and turned to scan the beast his curse included.

The little man looked down between the melancholy ears of his steed.

'I did my best,' he said.

The two others stared again across the valley for a space. The gaunt man passed the back of his hand across the scarred lip.

'Come up!' said the man who owned the silver bridle, suddenly. The little man started and jerked his rein, and the horse hoofs of the three made a multitudinous faint pattering upon the withered grass as they turned back towards the trail. . . .

They rode cautiously down the long slope before them, and so came through a waste of prickly twisted bushes and strange dry shapes of horny branches that grew amongst the rocks, into the level below. And there the trail grew faint, for the soil was scanty, and the only herbage was this scorched dead straw that lay upon the ground. Still, by hard scanning, by leaning beside the horse's neck and pausing ever and again, even these white men could contrive to follow after their prey.

There were trodden places, bent and broken blades of the coarse grass, and ever and again the sufficient intimation of a footmark. And once the leader saw a brown smear of blood where the half-caste girl may have trod. And at that under his breath he cursed her for a fool.

The gaunt man checked his leader's tracking, and the little man on the white horse rode behind, a man lost in a dream. They rode one after another, the man with the silver bridle led the way, and they spoke never a word. After a time it came to the little man on the white horse that the world was very still. He started out of his dream. Besides the minute noises of their horses and equipment, the whole great valley kept the brooding quiet of a painted scene.

Before him went his master and his fellow, each intently leaning forward to the left, each impassively moving with the paces of his horse; their shadows went before them—still, noiseless, tapering attendants; and nearer a crouched cool shape was his own. He looked about him. What was it had gone? Then he remembered the reverberation from the banks of the gorge and the perpetual accompaniment of shifting, jostling pebbles. And, moreover——? There was no breeze. That was it! What a vast, still place it was, a monotonous afternoon slumber. And the sky open and blank, except for a sombre veil of haze that had gathered in the upper valley.

He straightened his back, fretted with his bridle, puckered his lips to whistle, and simply sighed. He turned in his saddle for a time, and stared at the throat of the mountain gorge out of which they had come. Blank! Blank slopes on either side, with never a sign of a decent beast or tree—much less a man. What a land it was! What a wilderness! He dropped again into his former pose.

It filled him with a momentary pleasure to see a wry stick of purple black flash out into the form of a snake, and vanish amidst the brown. After all, the infernal valley *was* alive. And then, to rejoice him still more, came a breath across his face, a whisper that came and went, the faintest inclination of a stiff black-antlered bush upon a crest, the first intimations of a possible breeze. Idly he whetted his finger, and held it up.

He pulled up sharply to avoid a collision with the gaunt man, who had stopped at fault upon the trail. Just at that guilty moment he caught his master's eye looking towards him.

For a time he forced an interest in the tracking. Then, as they rode on again, he studied his master's shadow and hat and shoulder appearing and disappearing behind the gaunt man's nearer contours. They had ridden four days out of the very limits of the world into this desolate place, short of water, with nothing but a strip of dried meat under their saddles, over rocks and mountains, where surely none but these fugitives had ever been before—for *that*!

And all this was for a girl, a mere wilful child! And the man had whole cityfuls of people to do his basest bidding—girls, women! Why in the name of passionate folly *this* one in particular? asked the little man, and scowled at the world, and licked his parched lips with a blackened tongue. It was the way of the master, and that was all he knew. Just because she sought to evade him. . . .

His eye caught a whole row of high plumed canes bending in unison, and then the tails of silk that hung before his neck flapped and fell. The breeze was growing stronger. Somehow it took the stiff stillness out of things—and that was well.

'Hullo!' said the gaunt man.

All three stopped abruptly.

'What?' asked the master. 'What?'

'Over there,' said the gaunt man, pointing up the valley.

'What?'

'Something coming towards us.'

And as he spoke a yellow animal crested a rise and came bearing down upon them. It was a big wild dog, coming before the wind, tongue out, at a steady pace, and running with such an intensity of purpose that he did not seem to see the horsemen he approached. He ran with his nose up, following, it was plain, neither scent nor quarry. As he drew nearer the little man felt for his sword. 'He's mad,' said the gaunt rider.

'Shout!' said the little man and shouted.

The dog came on. Then when the little man's blade was already out, it swerved aside and went panting by them and past. The eyes of the little man followed its flight. 'There was no foam,' he said. For a space the man with the silver-studded bridle stared up the valley. 'Oh, come on!' he cried at last. 'What does it matter?' and jerked his horse into movement again.

The little man left the insoluble mystery of a dog that fled from nothing but the wind, and lapsed into profound musings on human character. 'Come on!' he whispered to himself. 'Why should it be given to one man to say "Come on!" with that stupendous violence of effect. Always, all his life, the man with the silver bridle has been saying that. If *I* said it——!' thought

25

the little man. But people marvelled when the master was disobeyed even in the wildest things. This half-caste girl seemed to him, seemed to everyone, mad—blasphemous almost. The little man, by way of comparison, reflected on the gaunt rider with the scarred lip, as stalwart as his master, as brave and, indeed, perhaps braver, and yet for him there was obedience, nothing but to give obedience duly and stoutly. . . .

Certain sensations of the hands and knees called the little man back to more immediate things. He became aware of something. He rode up beside his gaunt fellow. 'Do you notice the horses?' he said in an undertone.

The gaunt face looked interrogation.

'They don't like this wind,' said the little man, and dropped behind as the man with the silver bridle turned upon him.

'It's all right,' said the gaunt-faced man.

They rode on again for a space in silence. The foremost two rode downcast upon the trail, the hindmost man watched the haze that crept down the vastness of the valley, nearer and nearer, and noted how the wind grew in strength moment by moment. Far away on the left he saw a line of dark bulks—wild hog perhaps, galloping down the valley, but of that he said nothing, nor did he remark again upon the uneasiness of the horses.

And then he saw first one and then a second great white ball, a great shining white ball like a gigantic head of thistledown, that drove before the wind athwart the path. These balls soared high in the air, and dropped and rose again and caught for a moment, and hurried on and passed, but at the sight of them the restlessness of the horses increased.

Then presently he saw that more of these drifting globes—and then soon very many more—were hurrying towards him down the valley.

26

They became aware of a squealing. Athwart the path a huge boar rushed, turning his head but for one instant to glance at them, and then hurtling on down the valley again. And at that, all three stopped and sat in their saddles, staring into the thickening haze that was coming upon them.

'If it were not for this thistledown—' began the leader.

But now a big globe came drifting past within a score of yards of them. It was really not an even sphere at all, but a vast, soft, ragged, filmy thing, a sheet gathered by the corners, an aerial jelly-fish, as it were, but rolling over and over as it advanced, and trailing long, cob-webby threads and streamers that floated in its wake.

'It isn't thistledown,' said the little man.

'I don't like the stuff,' said the gaunt man.

And they looked at one another.

'Curse it!' cried the leader. 'The air's full of it up there. If it keeps on at this pace long, it will stop us altogether.'

An instinctive feeling, such as lines out a herd of deer at the approach of some ambiguous thing, prompted them to turn their horses to the wind, ride forwards for a few paces, and stare at that advancing multitude of floating masses. They came on before the wind with a sort of smooth swiftness, rising and falling noiselessly, sinking to earth, rebounding high, soaring—all with a perfect unanimity, with a still, deliberate assurance.

Right and left of the horsemen the pioneers of this strange army passed. At one that rolled along the ground, breaking shapelessly and trailing out reluctantly into long grappling ribbons and bands, all three horses began to shy and dance. The master was seized with a sudden, unreasonable impatience. He cursed the drifting globes roundly. 'Get on!' he cried; 'get on! What do these things matter? How *can* they matter? Back to the trail!' He fell swearing at his horse and sawed the bit across its mouth.

He shouted aloud with rage. 'I will follow that trail, I tell you,' he cried. 'Where is the trail!'

He gripped the bridle of his prancing horse and searched amidst the grass. A long and clinging thread fell across his face, a grey streamer dropped about his bridle arm, some big, active thing with many legs ran down the back of his head. He looked up to discover one of those grey masses anchored as it were above him by these things and flapping out ends as a sail flaps when a boat comes about—but noiselessly.

He had an impression of many eyes, of a dense crew of squat bodies, of long, many-jointed limbs hauling at their mooring ropes to bring the thing down upon him. For a space he stared up, reining in his prancing horse with the instinct born of years of horsemanship. Then the flat of a sword smote his back, and a blade flashed overhead and cut the drifting balloon of spider-web free, and the whole mass lifted softly and drove clear and away.

'Spiders!' cried the voice of the gaunt man. 'The things are full of big spiders! Look, my lord!'

The man with the silver bridle still followed the mass that drove away.

'Look, my lord!'

The master found himself staring down at a red smashed thing on the ground that, in spite of partial obliteration, could still wriggle unavailing legs. Then when the gaunt man pointed to another mass that bore down upon them, he drew his sword hastily. Up the valley now it was like a fog bank torn to rags. He tried to grasp the situation.

'Ride for it!' the little man was shouting. 'Ride for it down the valley.'

What happened then was like the confusion of a battle. The man with the silver bridle saw the little man go past him slashing furiously at imaginary cobwebs, saw him cannon into the horse of the gaunt man and hurl it and its rider to earth. His own horse went a dozen paces before he could rein it in. Then he looked up to avoid imaginary dangers, and then back again to see a horse rolling on the ground, the gaunt man standing and slashing over it at a rent and fluttering mass of grey that streamed and wrapped about them both. And thick and fast as thistledown on waste land on a windy day in July, the cobweb masses were coming on.

The little man had dismounted, but he dared not release his horse. He was endeavouring to lug the struggling brute back with the strength of one arm, while with the other he slashed aimlessly. The tentacles of a second grey mass had entangled themselves with the struggle, and this second grey mass came to its moorings, and slowly sank.

The master set his teeth, gripped his bridle, lowered his head, and spurred his horse forward. The horse on the ground rolled over, there was blood and moving shapes upon the flanks, and the gaunt man suddenly leaving it, ran forward towards his master, perhaps ten paces. His legs were swathed and encumbered with grey; he made ineffectual movements with his sword. Grey streamers waved from him; there was a thin veil of grey across his face. With his left hand he beat at something on his body, and suddenly he stumbled and fell. He struggled to rise, and fell again, and suddenly, horribly, began to howl, 'Oh—ohoo- ohooh!'

The master could see the great spiders upon him, and others upon the ground.

As he strove to force his horse nearer to this gesticulating screaming grey object that struggled up and down,

The man with the silver bridle rode . . . his sword
arm ready to slash

there came a clatter of hoofs, and the little man, in act of mounting, swordless, balanced on his belly athwart the white horse, and clutching its mane, whirled past. And again a clinging thread of grey gossamer swept across the master's face. All about him and over him, it seemed this drifting, noiseless cobweb circled and drew nearer him. . . .

To the day of his death he never knew just how the event of that moment happened. Did he, indeed, turn his horse, or did it really of its own accord stampede after its fellow? Suffice it that in another second he was galloping full tilt down the valley with his sword whirling furiously overhead. And all about him on the quickening breeze, the spiders' airships, their air bundles and air sheets, seemed to him to hurry in a conscious pursuit.

Clatter, clatter, thud, thud—the man with the silver bridle rode, heedless of his direction, with his fearful face looking up now right, now left, and his sword arm ready to slash. And a few hundred yards ahead of him, with a tail of torn cobweb trailing behind him, rode the little man on the white horse, still but imperfectly in the saddle. The reeds bent before them, the wind blew fresh and strong, over his shoulder the master could see the webs hurrying to overtake. . . .

He was so intent to escape the spiders' webs that only as his horse gathered together for a leap did he realise the ravine ahead. And then he realized it only to misunderstand and interfere. He was leaning forward on his horse's neck and sat up and back all too late.

But if in his excitement he had failed to leap, at any rate he had not forgotten how to fall. He was a horseman again in mid-air. He came off clear with a mere bruise upon his shoulder, and his horse rolled, kicking spasmodic legs, and lay still. But the master's sword drove its point into the hard soil, and snapped clean across, as though Chance refused him any longer as her Knight, and the splintered end missed his face by an inch or so.

He was on his feet in a moment, breathlessly scanning the onrushing spider-webs. For a moment he was minded to run, and then thought of the ravine, and turned back. He ran aside once to dodge one drifting terror, and then he was swiftly clambering down the precipitous sides, and out of the touch of the gale.

There under the lee of the dry torrent's steeper banks he might crouch, and watch these strange, grey masses pass and pass in safety till the wind fell, and it became possible to escape. And there for a long time he crouched, watching the strange, grey, ragged masses trail their streamers across his narrowed sky.

Once a stray spider fell into the ravine close beside him—a full foot it measured from leg to leg, and its body was half a man's hand—and after he had watched its monstrous alacrity of search and escape for a little while, and tempted it to bite his broken sword, he lifted up his iron heeled boot and smashed it into a pulp. He swore as he did so, and for a time sought up and down for another.

Then presently, when he was surer these spider swarms could not drop into the ravine, he found a place where he could sit down, and sat and fell into deep thought and began after his manner to gnaw his knuckles and bite his nails. And from this he was moved by the coming of the man with the white horse.

He heard him long before he saw him as a clattering of hoofs, stumbling footsteps, and a reassuring voice. Then the little man appeared, a rueful figure, still with a tail of white cobweb trailing behind him. They approached each other without speaking, without a salutation. The little man was fatigued and shamed to the pitch of hopeless bitterness, and came to a stop at last, face to face with his seated master. The latter winced a little under his dependant's eye. 'Well?' he said at last, with no pretence of authority.

'You left him!'

'My horse bolted.'

'I know. So did mine.'

He laughed at his master mirthlessly.

'I say my horse bolted,' said the man who once had a silver-studded bridle.

'Cowards both,' said the little man.

The other gnawed his knuckle through some meditative moments, with his eyes on his inferior.

'Don't call me a coward,' he said at length.

'You are a coward like myself.'

'A coward possibly. There is a limit beyond which every man must fear. That I have learnt at last. But not like yourself. That is where the difference comes in.'

'I never could have dreamt you would have left him. He saved your life two minutes before. . . . Why are you our lord?'

The master gnawed his knuckles again, and his countenance was dark.

'No man calls me a coward,' he said. 'No. . . . A broken sword is better than none. . . . One spavined white horse cannot be expected to carry two men a four days' journey. I hate white horses, but this time it cannot be helped. You begin to understand me? . . . I perceive that you are minded, on the strength of what you have seen and fancy, to taint my reputation. It is men of your sort who unmake kings. Besides which—I never liked you.'

'My lord!' said the little man.

'No,' said the master. '*No!*'

He stood up sharply as the little man moved. For a minute perhaps they faced one another. Overhead the spiders' balls went driving. There was a quick movement among the pebbles; a running of feet, a cry of despair, a gasp and a blow. . . .

Towards nightfall the wind fell. The sun set in a calm serenity, and the man who had once possessed the silver bridle came at last very cautiously and by an easy slope out of the ravine again; but now he led the white horse that once belonged to the little man. He would have gone back to his horse to get his silver-mounted bridle again, but he feared night and a quickening breeze might still find him in the valley, and besides he disliked greatly to think he might discover his horse all swathed in cobwebs and perhaps unpleasantly eaten.

And as he thought of those cobwebs and of all the dangers he had been through, and the manner in which he had been preserved that day, his hand sought a little reliquary that hung about his neck, and he clasped it for a moment with heartfelt gratitude. As he did so his eyes went across the valley.

'I was hot with passion,' he said, 'and now she has met her reward. They also, no doubt——'

And behold! Far away out of the wooded slopes across the valley, but in the clearness of the sunset distinct and unmistakable, he saw a little spire of smoke.

At that his expression of serene resignation changed to an amazed anger. Smoke? He turned the head of the white horse about, and hesitated. And as he did so a little rustle of air went through the grass about him. Far away upon some reeds swayed a tattered sheet of grey. He looked at the cobwebs; he looked at the smoke.

'Perhaps, after all, it is not them,' he said at last.

But he knew better.

After he had stared at the smoke for some time, he mounted the white horse.

As he rode, he picked his way amidst stranded masses of web. For some reason there were many dead spiders on the ground, and those that lived feasted guiltily on their fellow. At the sound of his horse's hoofs they fled.

Their time had passed. From the ground, without either a wind to carry them or a winding sheet ready, these things, for all their poison, could do him no evil.

He flicked with his belt at those he fancied came too near. Once, where a number ran together over a bare place, he was minded to dismount and trample them with his boots, but this impulse he overcame. Ever and again he turned in his saddle, and looked back at the smoke.

'Spiders,' he muttered over and over again. 'Spiders! Well, well. . . . The next time I must spin a web.'

GOOD COMPANY

Leonard Clark

I sleep in a room at the top of the house
With a flea, and a fly, and a soft-scratching mouse,
And a spider who hangs by a thread from the ceiling,
Who gives me each day such a curious feeling
When I watch him at work on the beautiful weave
Of his web that's so fine I can hardly believe
It won't all end up in such terrible tangles,
For he sways as he weaves, and spins as he dangles.
I cannot get up to that spider, I know,
And I hope he won't get down to me here below,
And yet when I wake in the chill morning air
I'd miss him if he were not still swinging there,
For I have in my room such good company,
There's him, and the mouse, and the fly, and the flea.

Snakes

The Legend of Cadmus

Thomas Bullfinch

The myth of Cadmus concerns an encounter between a man and a terrible snake.

Jupiter, under the disguise of a bull, had carried away Europa, the daughter of Agenor, king of Phoenicia. Agenor commanded his son Cadmus to go in search of his sister, and not to return without her. Cadmus went and sought long and far for his sister, but could not find her, and not daring to return unsuccessful, consulted the Oracle of Apollo to know what country he should settle in. The Oracle informed him that he should find a cow in the field, and should follow her wherever she might wander, and where she stopped, should build a city and call it Thebes.

Cadmus had hardly left the Castalian cave, from which the oracle was delivered, when he saw a young cow slowly walking before him. He followed her close, offering at the same time his prayers to Phoebus. The cow went on till she passed the shallow channel of Cephisus and came out into the plain of Panope. There she stood still, and raising her broad forehead to the sky, filled the air with her lowings. Cadmus gave thanks, and stooping down kissed the foreign soil, then lifting his eyes, greetcd the surrounding mountains. Wishing to offer a sacrifice to Jupiter, he sent his servants to seek pure water for a libation.

Near by there stood an ancient grove which had never been profaned by the axe, in the midst of which was a cave, thick covered with the growth of bushes, its roof forming a low arch, from beneath which burst forth a fountain of purest water. In the cave lurked a horrid serpent with a crested head and scales glittering like gold. His eyes shone like fire, his body was swollen with venom, he vibrated a triple tongue, and showed a triple row of teeth. No sooner had the Tyrians dipped their pitchers in the fountain, and the in-gushing waters made a sound, than the glittering serpent raised his head out of the cave and uttered a fearful hiss. The vessels fell from their hands, the blood left their cheeks, they trembled in every limb. The serpent, twisting his scaly body in a huge coil, raised his head so as to overtop the tallest trees, and while the Tyrians from terror could neither fight nor fly, slew some with his fangs, others in his folds, and others with his poisonous breath.

Cadmus, having waited for the return of his men till midday, went in search of them. His covering was a lion's hide, and besides his javelin he carried in his hand a lance, and in his breast a bold heart, a surer reliance than either. When he entered the wood, and saw the lifeless bodies of his men, and the monster with his bloody jaws, he exclaimed, 'O faithful friends, I will avenge you, or share your death.' So saying he lifted a huge stone and threw it with all his force at the serpent. Such a block would have shaken the wall of a fortress, but it made no impression on the monster. Cadmus next threw his javelin, which met with better success, for it penetrated the serpent's scales, and pierced through to his entrails. Fierce with pain, the monster turned back his head to view the wound, and attempted to draw out the weapon with his mouth, but broke it off, leaving the iron point rankling in his flesh. His neck swelled with rage, bloody foam covered his jaws, and the breath of his nostrils poisoned the air around. Now he twisted himself into a circle, then stretched himself out on the ground like the trunk of a fallen tree. As he moved onward, Cadmus retreated before him, holding his spear opposite to the monster's opened jaws. The serpent snapped at the weapon and attempted to bite its iron point. At last Cadmus, watching his chance, thrust the spear at a moment when the animal's head thrown back came against the trunk of a tree, and so succeeded in pinning him to its side. His weight bent the tree as he struggled in the agonies of death.

While Cadmus stood over his conquered foe, contemplating its vast size, a voice was heard (from whence he knew not, but he heard it distinctly) commanding him to take the dragon's teeth and sow them in the earth. He obeyed. He made a furrow in the ground, and planted the teeth, destined to produce a crop of men. Scarce had he done so when the clods began to move, and the points of spears began to appear above the surface. Next, helmets with their nodding plumes came up, and next the shoulders and breasts and limbs of men with weapons, and in time a harvest of armed warriors. Cadmus, alarmed, prepared to encounter a new enemy, but one of them said to him, 'Meddle not with our civil war.' With that he who had spoken smote one of his earth-born brothers with a sword, and he himself fell pierced with an arrow from another. The latter fell victim to a fourth, and in like manner the whole crowd dealt with each other till all fell, slain with mutual wounds, except five survivors. One of these cast away his weapons and said, 'Brothers, let us live in peace!' These five joined Cadmus in building his city, to which they gave the name of Thebes.

Cadmus obtained in marriage Harmonia, the daughter of Venus. The gods left Olympus to honour the occasion with their presence, and Vulcan presented the bride with a necklace of surpassing brilliancy, his own workmanship. But a fatality hung over the family of Cadmus in consequence of his killing of the serpent sacred to Mars. Semele and Ino, his daughters, and Actaeon and Pentheus, his grand-children, all perished unhappily, and Cadmus and Harmonia quitted Thebes, now grown odious to them, and emigrated to the country of the Enchelians, who received them with honour and made Cadmus their king. But the misfortunes of their children still weighed on their minds; and one day Cadmus exclaimed, 'If a serpent's life is so dear to the gods, I would I were myself a serpent.' No sooner had he uttered these words than he began to change his form. Harmonia beheld it and prayed to the gods to let her share his fate. Both became serpents. They live in the woods, but mindful of their origin, they neither avoid the presence of man nor do they ever injure anyone.

"Rikki-Tikki-Tavi"

Rudyard Kipling

This is the story of the great war that Rikki-tikki-tavi fought single-handed, through the bath-rooms of the big bungalow in Segowlee cantonment. Darzee, the tailor-bird, helped him, and Chuchundra, the muskrat, who never comes out into the middle of the floor, but always creeps round by the wall, gave him advice; but Rikki-tikki did the real fighting.

He was a mongoose, rather like a little cat in his fur and his tail, but quite like a weasel in his head and his habits. His eyes and the end of his restless nose were pink; he could scratch himself anywhere he pleased, with any leg, front or back, that he chose to use; he could fluff up his tail till it looked like a bottle-brush, and his war-cry as he scuttled through the long grass, was: '*Rikk-tikk-tikki-tikki-tchk!*'

One day, a high summer flood washed him out of the burrow where he lived with his father and mother, and carried him, kicking and clucking, down a roadside ditch. He found a little wisp of grass floating there, and clung to it till he lost his senses. When he revived, he was lying in the hot sun on the middle of a garden path, very draggled indeed, and a small boy was saying: 'Here's a dead mongoose. Let's have a funeral.'

'No,' said his mother; 'let's take him in and dry him. Perhaps he isn't really dead.'

They took him into the house, and a big man picked him up between his finger and thumb and said he was not dead but half choked; so they wrapped him in cotton-wool, and warmed him, and he opened his eyes and sneezed.

'Now,' said the big man (he was an Englishman who had just moved into the bungalow); 'don't frighten him, and we'll see what he'll do.'

It is the hardest thing in the world to frighten a mongoose, because he is eaten up from nose to tail with curiosity. The motto of all the mongoose family is 'Run and find out'; and Rikki-tikki was a true mongoose. He looked at the cotton-wool, decided that it was not

Rikki-Tikki looked down between the boy's collar and neck.

good to eat, ran all round the table, sat up and put his fur in order, scratched himself, and jumped on the small boy's shoulder.

'Don't be frightened, Teddy,' said his father. 'That's his way of making friends.'

'Ouch! He's tickling under my chin,' said Teddy.

Rikki-tikki looked down between the boy's collar and neck, snuffed at his ear, and climbed down to the floor, where he sat rubbing his nose.

'Good gracious,' said Teddy's mother, 'and that's a wild creature! I suppose he's so tame because we've been kind to him.'

'All mongooses are like that,' said her husband. 'If Teddy doesn't pick him up by the tail, or try to put him in a cage, he'll run in and out of the house all day long. Let's give him something to eat.'

They gave him a little piece of raw meat. Rikki-tikki liked it immensely, and when it was finished he went

He put his nose into the ink.

out into the veranda and sat in the sunshine and fluffed up his fur to make it dry to the roots. Then he felt better.

'There are more things to find out about in this house,' he said to himself, 'than all my family could find out in all their lives. I shall certainly stay and find out.'

He spent all that day roaming over the house. He nearly drowned himself in the bath-tubs, put his nose into the ink on a writing-table, and burned it on the end of the big man's cigar, for he climbed up in the big man's lap to see how writing was done. At nightfall he ran into Teddy's nursery to watch how kerosene lamps were lighted, and when Teddy went to bed Rikki-tikki climbed up too; but he was a restless companion, because he had to get up and attend to every noise all through the night, and find out what made it. Teddy's mother and father came in, the last thing, to look at their boy, and Rikki-tikki was awake on the pillow. 'I don't like that,' said Teddy's mother; 'he may bite the child.' 'He'll do no such thing,' said the father. 'Teddy's safer with that little beast than if he had a bloodhound to watch him. If a snake came into the nursery now—'

Rikki-Tikki was awake on the pillow.

But Teddy's mother wouldn't think of anything so awful.

Early in the morning Rikki-tikki came to early breakfast in the veranda riding on Teddy's shoulder, and they gave him banana and some boiled egg; and he sat on all their laps one after the other, because every well-brought-up mongoose always hopes to be a house-mongoose some day and have rooms to run about in, and Rikki-tikki's mother (she used to live in the General's house at Segowlee) had carefully told Rikki what to do if he ever came across white men.

Then Rikki-tikki went out into the garden to see what was to be seen. It was a large garden, only half cultivated, with bushes as big as summer houses of Marshal Niel roses, lime and orange trees, clumps of bamboos, and thickets of grass. Rikki-tikki licked his lips. 'This is a splendid hunting-ground,' he said, and his tail grew

He came to breakfast riding on Teddy's shoulder.

bottle-brushy at the thought of it, and he scuttled up and down the garden, snuffing here and there till he heard very sorrowful voices in a thorn-bush.

It was Darzee, the tailor-bird, and his wife. They had made a beautiful nest by pulling two big leaves together and stitching them up the edges with fibres, and had filled the hollow with cotton and downy fluff. The nest swayed to and fro, as they sat on the rim and cried. 'What is the matter?' asked Rikki-tikki.

'We are very miserable,' said Darzee. 'One of our babies fell out of the nest yesterday and Nag ate him.'

'H'm!' said Rikki-tikki, 'that is very sad—but I am a stranger here. Who is Nag?'

Darzee and his wife only cowered down in the nest without answering, for from the thick grass at the foot of the bush there came a low hiss—a horrid cold sound that made Rikki-tikki jump back two clear feet. Then inch by inch out of the grass rose up the head and spread hood of Nag, the big black cobra, and he was five feet long from tongue to tail. When he had lifted one-third of himself clear of the ground, he stayed balancing to and fro exactly as a dandelion-tuft balances in the wind, and he looked at Rikki-tikki with the wicked snake's eyes that never change their expression, whatever the snake may be thinking of.

'We are very miserable,' said Darzee.

'Who is Nag?' he said '*I* am Nag. The great God Brahm put his mark upon all our people when the first cobra spread his hood to keep the sun off Brahm as he slept. Look, and be afraid!'

He spread out his hood more than ever, and Rikki-tikki saw the spectacle-mark on the back of it that looks exactly like the eye part of a hook-and-eye fastening. He was afraid for the minute; but it is impossible for a

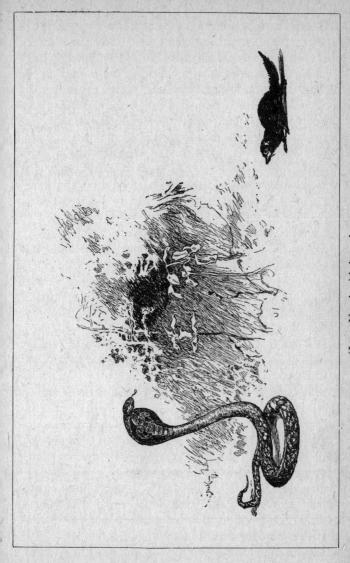

'I am Nag,' said the cobra . . .

mongoose to stay frightened for any length of time, and though Rikki-tikki had never met a live cobra before, his mother had fed him on dead ones, and he knew that all a grown mongoose's business in life was to fight and eat snakes. Nag knew that too, and at the bottom of his cold heart he was afraid.

'Well,' said Rikki-tikki, and his tail began to fluff up again, 'marks or no marks, do you think it is right for you to eat fledglings out of a nest?'

Nag was thinking to himself, and watching the least little movement in the grass behind Rikki-tikki. He knew that mongooses in the garden meant death sooner or later for him and his family; but he wanted to get Rikki-tikki off his guard. So he dropped his head a little, and put it on one side.

'Let us talk,' he said. 'You eat eggs. Why should not I eat birds?'

'Behind you! Look behind you!' sang Darzee.

Rikki-tikki knew better than to waste time in staring. He jumped up in the air as high as he could go, and just under him whizzed by the head of Nagaina, Nag's wicked wife. She had crept up behind him as he was talking, to make an end of him; and he heard her savage hiss as the stroke missed. He came down almost across her back, and if he had been an old mongoose he would have known that then was the time to break her back with one bite; but he was afraid of the terrible lashing return-stroke of the cobra. He bit, indeed, but did not bite long enough, and he jumped clear of the whisking tail, leaving Nagaina torn and angry.

'Wicked, wicked Darzee!' said Nag, lashing up as high as he could reach toward the nest in the thorn-bush; but Darzee had built it out of reach of snakes, and it only swayed to and fro.

Rikki-tikki felt his eyes growing red and hot (when a

He jumped up in the air . . . .

mongoose's eyes grow red, he is angry), and he sat back on his tail and hind legs like a little kangaroo, and looked all around him, and chattered with rage. But Nag and Nagaina had disappeared into the grass. When a snake misses its stroke, it never says anything or gives any sign of what it means to do next. Rikki-tikki did not care to follow them, for he did not feel sure that he could manage two snakes at once. So he trotted off to the gravel path near the house, and sat down to think. It was a serious matter for him.

If you read the old books of natural history, you will find they say that when the mongoose fights the snake and happens to get bitten, he runs off and eats some herb that cures him. That is not true. The victory is only a matter of quickness of eye and quickness of foot, —snake's blow against mongoose's jump,—and as no eye can follow the motion of a snake's head when it strikes, that makes things much more wonderful than any magic herb. Rikki-tikki knew he was a young mongoose, and it made him all the more pleased to think that he had managed to escape a blow from behind. It gave him confidence in himself, and when Teddy came running down the path, Rikki-tikki was ready to be petted.

But just as Teddy was stooping, something flinched a little in the dust, and a tiny voice said: 'Be careful. I am death!' It was Karait, the dusty brown snakeling that lies for choice on the dusty earth; and his bite is as dangerous as the cobra's. But he is so small that nobody thinks of him, and so he does the more harm to people.

Rikki-tikki's eyes grew red again, and he danced up to Karait with the peculiar rocking, swaying motion that he had inherited from his family. It looks very funny, but it is so perfectly balanced a gait that you can fly off from it at any angle you please; and in dealing with snakes this is an advantage. If Rikki-tikki had only known, he was doing a much more dangerous thing than fighting Nag, for Karait is so small, and can turn so quickly, that unless Rikki bit him close to the back of the head, he would get the return-stroke in his eye or lip. But Rikki did not know: his eyes were all red, and he rocked back and forth, looking for a good place to hold. Karait struck out. Rikki jumped sideways and tried to run in, but the wicked little dusty grey head lashed within a fraction of his shoulder, and he had to jump over the body, and the head followed his heels close.

Teddy shouted to the house: 'Oh, look here! Our mongoose is killing a snake'; and Rikki-tikki heard a scream from Teddy's mother. His father ran out with a stick, but by the time he came up, Karait had lunged out once too far, and Rikki-tikki had sprung, jumped on the snake's back, dropped his head far between his fore legs, bitten as high up the back as he could get hold, and rolled away. That bite paralyzed Karait, and Rikki-tikki was just going to eat him up from the tail, after the custom of his family at dinner, when he remembered that a full meal makes a slow mongoose, and if he wanted all his strength and quickness ready, he must keep himself thin.

He went away for a dust-bath under the castor-oil bushes, while Teddy's father beat the dead Karait. 'What is the use of that?' thought Rikki-tikki. 'I have settled it all'; and then Teddy's mother picked him up from the dust and hugged him, crying that he had saved Teddy from death, and Teddy's father said that he was a providence, and Teddy looked on with big scared eyes. Rikki-tikki was rather amused at all the fuss, which, of course, he did not understand. Teddy's mother might just as well have petted Teddy for

53

playing in the dust. Rikki was thoroughly enjoying himself.

That night, at dinner, walking to and fro among the wine-glasses on the table, he could have stuffed himself three times over with nice things; but he remembered Nag and Nagaina, and though it was very pleasant to be patted and petted by Teddy's mother, and to sit on Teddy's shoulder, his eyes would get red from time

In the dark he ran up against Chuchundra, the musk-rat.

to time, and he would go off into his long war cry of '*Rikk-tikk-tikki-tikki-tchk!*'

Teddy carried him off to bed, and insisted on Rikki-tikki sleeping under his chin. Rikki-tikki was too well bred to bite or scratch, but as soon as Teddy was asleep he went off for his nightly walk round the house, and in the dark he ran up against Chuchundra, the muskrat, creeping round by the wall. Chuchundra is a brokenhearted little beast. He whimpers and cheeps all the night, trying to make up his mind to run into the middle of the room, but he never gets there.

'Don't kill me,' said Chuchundra, almost weeping. 'Rikki-tikki, don't kill me.'

'Do you think a snake-killer kills muskrats?' said Rikki-tikki scornfully.

'Those who kill snakes get killed by snakes,' said Chuchundra, more sorrowfully than ever.

'And how am I to be sure that Nag won't mistake me for you some dark night?'

'There's not the least danger,' said Rikki-tikki; 'but Nag is in the garden, and I know you don't go there.'

'My cousin Chua, the rat, told me—' said Chuchundra, and then he stopped.

'Told you what?'

'H'sh! Nag is everywhere, Rikki-tikki. You should have talked to Chua in the garden.'

'I didn't—so you must tell me. Quick, Chuchundra, or I'll bite you!'

Chuchundra sat down and cried till the tears rolled off his whiskers. 'I am a very poor man,' he sobbed. 'I never had spirit enough to run out into the middle of the room. H'sh! I musn't tell you anything. Can't you *hear*, Rikki-tikki?'

Rikki-tikki listened. The house was as still as still, but he thought he could just catch the faintest *scratch-scratch* in the world,—a noise as faint as that of a wasp walking on a window-pane,—the dry scratch of a snake's scales on brickwork.

'That's Nag or Nagaina,' he said to himself; 'and he is crawling into the bath-room sluice. You're right, Chuchundra; I should have talked to Chua.'

He stole off to Teddy's bath-room, but there was nothing there, and then to Teddy's mother's bath-room.

55

At the bottom of the smooth plaster wall there was a brick pulled out to make a sluice for the bath-water, and as Rikki-tikki stole in by the masonry curb where the bath is put, he heard Nag and Nagaina whispering together outside in the moonlight.

'When the house is emptied of people,' said Nagaina to her husband, '*he* will have to go away, and then the garden will be our own again. Go in quietly, and remember that the big man who killed Karait is the first one to bite. Then come out and tell me, and we will hunt for Rikki-tikki together.'

'But are you sure that there is anything to be gained by killing the people?' said Nag.

'Everything. When there were no people in the bungalow, did we have any mongoose in the garden? So long as the bungalow is empty, we are king and queen of the garden; and remember that as soon as our eggs in the melon-bed hatch (as they may tomorrow), our children will need room and quiet.'

'I had not thought of that,' said Nag. 'I will go, but there is no need that we should hunt for Rikki-tikki afterward. I will kill the big man and his wife, and the child if I can, and come away quietly. Then the bungalow will be empty, and Rikki-tikki will go.'

Rikki-tikki tingled all over with rage and hatred at this, and then Nag's head came through the sluice, and his five feet of cold body followed it. Angry as he was, Rikki-tikki was very frightened as he saw the size of the big cobra. Nag coiled himself up, raised his head, and looked into the bath-room in the dark, and Rikki could see his eyes glitter.

'Now, if I kill him here, Nagaina will know; and if I fight him on the open floor, the odds are in his favour. What am I to do?' said Rikki-tikki-tavi.

Nag waved to and fro, and then Rikki-tikki heard

him drinking from the biggest water-jar that was used to fill the bath. 'That is good,' said the snake. 'Now, when Karait was killed, the big man had a stick. He may have that stick still, but when he comes in to bathe in the morning he will not have a stick. I shall wait here till he comes. Nagaina—do you hear me?—I shall wait here in the cool till daytime.'

There was no answer from outside, so Rikki-tikki knew Nagaina had gone away. Nag coiled himself down, coil by coil, round the bulge at the bottom of the water-jar, and Rikki-tikki stayed still as death. After an hour he began to move, muscle by muscle, toward the jar. Nag was asleep, and Rikki-tikki looked at his big back, wondering which would be the best place for a good hold. 'If I don't break his back at the first jump,' said Rikki, 'he can still fight; and if he fights—O Rikki!' He looked at the thickness of the neck below the hood, but that was too much for him; and a bite near the tail would only make Nag savage.

'It must be the head,' he said at last; 'the head above the hood; and, when I am once there I must not let go.'

Then he jumped. The head was lying a little clear of the water-jar, under the curve of it; and, as his teeth met, Rikki braced his back against the bulge of the red earthenware to hold down the head. This gave him just one second's purchase and he made the most of it. Then he was battered to and fro as a rat is shaken by a dog— to and fro on the floor, up and down, and round in great circles; but his eyes were red, and he held on as the body cartwhipped over the floor, upsetting the tin dipper and the soap-dish and the flesh-brush, and banged against the tin side of the bath. As he held he closed his jaws tighter and tighter, for he made sure he would be banged to death, and, for the honour of his family, he preferred to be found with his teeth locked. He was dizzy, aching, and felt shaken to pieces when something went off like a thunderclap just behind him; a hot wind knocked him senseless and red fire singed his fur. The big man had been wakened by the noise, and had fired both barrels of a shot-gun into Nag just behind the hood.

Rikki-tikki held on with his eyes shut, for now he was quite sure he was dead; but the head did not move, and

Then Rikki-Tikki was battered to and fro . . .

the big man picked him up and said: 'It's the mongoose again, Alice; the little chap has saved *our* lives now.' Then Teddy's mother came in with a very white face, and saw what was left of Nag, and Rikki-tikki dragged himself to Teddy's bedroom and spent half the rest of the night shaking himself tenderly to find out whether he really was broken into forty pieces, as he fancied.

When morning came he was very stiff, but well pleased with his doings. 'Now I have Nagaina to settle with, and she will be worse than five Nags, and there's no knowing when the eggs she spoke of will hatch. Goodness! I must go and see Darzee,' he said.

Without waiting for breakfast, Rikki-tikki ran to the thorn-bush where Darzee was singing a song of triumph at the top of his voice. The news of Nag's death was all over the garden, for the sweeper had thrown the body on the rubbish-heap.

'Oh, you stupid tuft of feathers!' said Rikki-tikki, angrily, 'Is this the time to sing?'

'Nag is dead—is dead—is dead!' sang Darzee. 'The valiant Rikki-tikki caught him by the head and held fast. The big man brought the bang-stick and Nag fell in two pieces! He will never eat my babies again.'

'All that's true enough; but where's Nagaina?' said Rikki-tikki, looking carefully round him.

'Nagaina came to the bath-room sluice and called for Nag,' Darzee went on; 'and Nag came out on the end of a stick—the sweeper picked him up on the end of a stick and threw him upon the rubbish-heap. Let us sing about the great, the red-eyed Rikki-tikki!' and Darzee filled his throat and sang.

'If I could get up to your nest, I'd roll all your babies out!' said Rikki-tikki. 'You don't know when to do the right thing at the right time. You're safe enough in your nest there, but it's war for me down here. Stop singing a minute, Darzee.'

'For the great, the beautiful Rikki-tikki's sake I will stop,' said Darzee. 'What is it, O Killer of the terrible Nag!'

'Where is Nagaina, for the third time?'

'On the rubbish-heap by the stables mourning for Nag. Great is Rikki-tikki with the white teeth.'

Darzee's wife pretends to have a broken wing.

'Bother my white teeth! Have you ever heard where she keeps her eggs?'

'In the melon-bed, on the end nearest the wall, where the sun strikes nearly all day. She had them there weeks ago.'

'And you never thought it worth while to tell me? The end nearest the wall, you said?'

'Rikki-tikki, you are not going to eat her eggs?'

'Not eat exactly; no. Darzee, if you have a grain of sense you will fly off to the stables and pretend that your wing is broken, and let Nagaina chase you away to this bush? I must get to the melon-bed, and if I went there now she'd see me.'

Darzee was a feather-brained little fellow who could never hold more than one idea at a time in his head; and just because he knew that Nagaina's children were born in eggs like his own, he didn't think at first that it was fair to kill them. But his wife was a sensible bird, and she knew that cobra's eggs meant young cobras later on; so she flew off from the nest, and left Darzee to keep the babies warm, and continue his song about the death of Nag. Darzee was very like a man in some ways.

She fluttered in front of Nagaina by the rubbish-heap, and cried out, 'Oh, my wing is broken! The boy in the house threw a stone at me and broke it.' Then she fluttered more desperately than ever.

Nagaina lifted up her head and hissed, 'You warned Rikki-tikki when I would have killed him. Indeed and truly, you've chosen a bad place to be lame in.' And she moved toward Darzee's wife, slipping along over the dust.

'The boy broke it with a stone!' shrieked Darzee's wife.

'Well! It may be some consolation to you when you're dead to know that I shall settle accounts with the boy.

My husband lies on the rubbish-heap this morning, but before night the boy in the house will lie very still. What is the use of running away? I am sure to catch you. Little fool, look at me!'

Darzee's wife knew better than to do *that*, for a bird who looks at a snake's eyes gets so frightened that she cannot move. Darzee's wife fluttered on, piping sorrowfully, and never leaving the ground, and Nagaina quickened her pace.

Rikki-tikki heard them going up the path from the stables, and he raced for the end of the melon-patch near the wall. There, in the warm litter about the melons, very cunningly hidden, he found twenty-five eggs, about the size of a bantam's eggs, but with whitish skin instead of shell.

'I was not a day too soon,' he said; for he could see the baby cobras curled up inside the skin, and he knew that the minute they were hatched they could each kill a man or a mongoose. He bit off the tops of the eggs as fast as he could, taking care to crush the young cobras, and turned over the litter from time to time to see whether he had missed any. At last there were only three eggs left, and Rikki-tikki began to chuckle to himself, when he heard Darzee's wife scraming:

'Rikki-tikki, I led Nagaina toward the house, and she has gone into the veranda, and—oh, come quickly— she means killing!'

Rikki-tikki smashed two eggs, and tumbled backward down the melon-bed with the third egg in his mouth, and scuttled to the veranda as hard as he could put foot to the ground. Teddy and his mother and father were there at early breakfast; but Rikki-tikki saw that they were not eating anything. They sat stone-still, and their faces were white. Nagaina was coiled up on the matting by Teddy's chair, within easy striking distance of Teddy's bare leg, and she was swaying to and fro singing a song of triumph.

'Son of the big man that killed Nag,' she hissed, 'stay still. I am not ready yet. Wait a little. Keep very still, all you three. If you move I strike, and if you do not move I strike. Oh, foolish people, who killed my Nag!'

Teddy's eyes were fixed on his father, and all his father could do was to whisper. 'Sit still, Teddy. You musn't move. Teddy, keep still.'

Then Rikki-tikki came up and cried: 'Turn round, Nagaina; turn and fight!'

'All in good time,' said she, without moving her eyes. 'I will settle my account with *you* presently. Look at your friends, Rikki-tikki. They are still and white; they are afraid. They dare not move, and if you come a step nearer I strike.'

'Look at your eggs,' said Rikki-tikki, 'in the melon-bed near the wall. Go and look Nagaina.'

The big snake turned half round, and saw the egg on the veranda. 'Ah-h! Give it to me,' she said.

Rikki-tikki put his paws on each side of the egg, and his eyes were blood-red. 'What price for a snake's egg? For a young cobra? For a young king-cobra? For the last—the very last of the brood? The ants are eating all the others down by the melon bed.'

Nagaina spun clear round, forgetting everything for the sake of the one egg; and Rikki-tikki saw Teddy's father shoot out a big hand, catch Teddy by the shoulder, and drag him across the little table with the tea-cups, safe and out of reach of Nagaina.

'Tricked! Tricked! Tricked! *Rikk-tck-tck!*' chuckled Rikki-tikki. 'The boy is safe, and it was I—I—I that caught Nag by the hood last night in the bath-room.' Then he began to jump up and down, all four feet together, his head close to the floor. 'He threw me to and fro, but he could not shake me off. He was dead before the big man blew him in two. I did it. *Rikki-tikki-tck-tck!* Come then, Nagaina. Come and fight with me. You shall not be a widow long.'

Nagaina saw that she had lost her chance of killing Teddy, and the

egg lay between Rikki-tikki's paws. 'Give me the egg, Rikki-tikki. Give me the last of my eggs, and I will go away and never come back,' she said, lowering her hood.

'Yes, you will go away, and you will never come back; for you will go to the rubbish-heap with Nag. Fight, widow! The big man has gone for his gun! Fight!'

Nagaina flew down the path, with Rikki-Tikki behind her.

Rikki-tikki was bounding all round Nagaina, keeping just out of reach of her stroke, his little eyes like hot coals. Nagaina gathered herself together, and flung out at him. Rikki-tikki jumped up and backward. Again and again she struck, and each time her head came with a whack

64

on the matting of the veranda and she gathered herself together like a watch-spring. Then Rikki-tikki danced in a circle to get behind her, and Nagaina spun round to keep her head to his head, so that the rustle of her tail on the matting sounded like dry leaves blown along by the wind.

He had forgotten the egg. It still lay on the veranda, and Nagaina came nearer and nearer to it, till at last, while Rikki-tikki was drawing breath, she caught it in her mouth, turned to the veranda steps, and flew like an arrow down the path, with Rikki-tikki behind her. When the cobra runs for her life, she goes like a whip-lash flicked across a horse's neck.

Rikki-tikki knew that he must catch her, or all the trouble would begin again. She headed straight for the long grass by the thorn-bush, and as he was running Rikki-tikki heard Darzee still singing his foolish little song of triumph. But Darzee's wife was wiser. She flew off her nest as Nagaina came along, and flapped her wings about Nagaina's head. If Darzee had helped they might have turned her; but Nagaina only lowered her hood and went on. Still, the instant's delay brought Rikki-tikki up to her, and as she plunged into the rat-hole where she and Nag used to live, his little white teeth were clenched on her tail, and he went down with her—and very few mongooses, however wise and old they may be, care to follow a cobra into its hole. It was dark in the hole; and Rikki-tikki never knew when it might open out and give Nagaina room to turn and strike at him. He held on savagely, and struck out his feet to act as brakes on the dark slope of the hot, moist earth.

Then the grass by the mouth of the hole stopped waving, and Darzee said: 'It is all over with Rikki-tikki! We must sing his deathsong. Valiant Rikki-tikki is dead! For Nagaina will surely kill him underground.'

So he sang a very mournful song that he made up all on the spur of the minute, and just as he got to the most touching part the grass quivered again, and Rikki-tikki, covered with dirt, dragged himself out of the hole leg by leg, licking his whiskers. Darzee stopped with a little shout. Rikki-tikki shook some of the dust out of his fur and sneezed. 'It is all over,' he said. 'The widow will

'It is all over.'

never come out again.' And the red ants that live between the grass stems heard him, and began to troop down one after another to see if he had spoken the truth.

Rikki-tikki curled himself up in the grass and slept where he was—slept and slept till it was late in the afternoon, for he had done a hard day's work.

'Now,' he said, when he awoke, 'I will go back to the

house. Tell the Coppersmith, Darzee, and he will tell the garden that Nagaina is dead.'

The Coppersmith is a bird who makes a noise exactly like the beating of a little hammer on a copper pot; and the reason he is always making it is because he is the town-crier to every Indian garden, and tells all the news to everybody who cares to listen. As Rikki-tikki went up the path, he heard his 'attention' notes like a tiny dinner-gong; and then the steady '*Ding-dong-tock!* Nag is dead —*dong!* Nagaina is dead! *Ding-dong-tock!*' That set all the birds in the garden singing, and the frogs croaking; for Nag and Nagaina used to eat frogs as well as little birds.

When Rikki got to the house, Teddy and Teddy's mother (she looked very white still, for she had been fainting) and Teddy's father came out and almost cried over him; and that night he ate all that was given him till he could eat no more, and went to bed on Teddy's shoulder, where Teddy's mother saw him when she came to look at night.

'He saved our lives and Teddy's life,' she said to her husband. 'Just think, he saved all our lives.'

Rikki-tikki woke up with a jump, for all the mongooses are light sleepers.

'Oh, it's you,' said he. 'What are you bothering for? All the cobras are dead; and if they weren't, I'm here.'

Rikki-tikki had a right to be proud of himself; but he did not grow too proud, and he kept that garden as a mongoose should keep it, with tooth and jump and spring and bite, till never a cobra dared show its head inside the walls.

Old Rattler and the King Snake

David Starr Jordan

'I only know thee humble, bold,
Haughty, with miseries untold,
And the old curse that left thee cold,
And drove thee ever to the sun
On blistering rocks. . . .
                    Thou whose fame
Searchest the grass with tongue of flame,
Making all creatures seem thy game,
When the whole woods before thee run,
Asked but—when all is said and done—
To lie, untrodden, in the sun!'—BRET HARTE.

Old Rattler was a snake, of course, and he lived in the
King's River Cañon, high up and down deep in the
mountains of California.

He had a hole behind and below a large, flat granite
rock, not far from the river, and he called it his home;
for in it he slept all night and all winter, but when the
sun came back in the spring and took the frost out of the
air and the rocks, then he crawled out to lie until he got
warm. The stream was clear and swift in the cañon, the
waterfalls sang in the side gulch of Roaring River, the

wind rustled in the long needles of the yellow pines, and the birds called to their mates in the branches. But Old Rattler did not care for such things. He was just a snake, you know, and his neighbours did not think him a good snake at that, for he was surly and silent, and his big, three-cornered, 'coffin-shaped' head, set on a slim, flat neck, was very ugly to see. But when he opened his mouth he was uglier still, for in his upper jaw he had two long fangs, and each one was filled with deadly poison. His vicious old head was covered with grey and wrinkled scales, and his black, beadlike eyes snapped when he opened his mouth to find out whether his fangs were both in working order.

Old Rattler was pretty stiff when he first came from his hole on the morning of this story. He had lain all night coiled up like a rope among the rocks, and his tail felt very cold. But the glad sun warmed the cockles of his heart, and in an hour or two he became limber, and this made him happy in his snaky fashion. But, being warm, he began to be hungry, for it had been a whole month since he had eaten anything. When the first new moon of August came, his skin loosened everywhere and slipped down over his eyes like a veil, so that he could see nothing about him, and could not hunt for frogs nor for chipmunks among the trees. But with the new moon of September all this was over. The rusty brown old coat was changed for a new suit of grey and black, and the diamond shaped chequers all over it were clean and shiny as a set of new clothes ought to be.

There was a little striped chipmunk running up and down the sugar-pine tree over his head, pursing his little mouth and throwing himself into pretty attitudes, as though he were the centre of an admiring audience, and Old Rattler kept a steady eye on him. But he was in no hurry about it all. He must first get the kinks out of his neck, and the cold cramps from his tail. There was an old curse on his family, so the other beasts had heard, that kept him always cold, and his tail was the coldest part of all. So he shook it a little, just to show that it was growing limber, and the bone clappers on the end rustled with a sharp, angry noise. Fifteen rattles he had in all—fifteen and a button—and to have so many showed that he was no common member of his hated family. Then he shook his tail again, and more sharply. This was to show all the world that he, Old Rattler, was wide awake, and whoever stepped on him would better look out. Then all the big beasts and little beasts who heard the noise fled away just as fast as ever they could; and to run away was the best thing they could do, for when Old Rattler struck one of them with his fangs all was over with him. So there were many in the cañon, beasts and birds and snakes too, who hated Old Rattler, but only a few dared face him. And one of these was Glittershield, whom men call the King of Snakes, and in a minute I shall tell you why.

And when Old Rattler was doing all that I have said, the King Snake lay low on a bed of pine needles, behind a bunch of fern, and watched with keen, sharp eye. The angry buzz of Rattler's tail, which scared the chipmunks and the bullfrogs and all the rest of the beast folk, was music for Glittershield. He was a snake too, and snakes understand some things better than any of the rest of us.

Glittershield was slim and wiry in his body, as long as Old Rattler himself, but was not so large around. His coat was smooth and glossy, not rough and wrinkly like Old Rattler's, and his up-raised head was small and pretty—for a snake. He was the best dressed of all his kind, and he looked his finest as he faced Old Rattler. His head was shiny black, his throat and neck as white as milk, while all down his body to the end of his tail he was painted with rings, first white, then black, then crimson, and every ring was bright as if it had just been freshly polished that very day.

So the King Snake passed the sheltering fern and came right up to Old Rattler. Rattler opened his sleepy eyes, threw himself on guard with a snap and a buzz, and shook his bony clappers savagely. But the King of Snakes was not afraid. Every snake has a weak spot somewhere, and that is the place to strike him. If he hadn't a weak spot no one else could live about him, and then perhaps he would starve to death at last. If he had not some strong points, where no one could harm him, he couldn't live himself.

As the black crest rose, Old Rattler's tail grew cold, his head dropped, his mouth closed, he straightened out his coil, and staggered helplessly toward his hole.

This was the chance for Glittershield. With a dash so swift that all the rings on his body—red, white, and black—melted into one purple flash, he seized Old Rattler by his throat. He carried no weapons, to be sure. He had neither fangs nor venom. He won his victories by force and dash, not by mean advantage. He was quick and strong, and his little hooked teeth held like the claws of a hawk. Old Rattler closed his mouth because he couldn't help it, and the fangs he could not use were folded back against the roof of his jaw.

The King Snake leaped forward, wound his body in a 'love-knot' around Old Rattler's neck, took a 'half-hitch' with his tail about the stomach, while the rest of his body lay in a curve like the letter S between the two knots. Then all he had to do was to stiffen up his muscles, and Old Rattler's backbone was snapped off at the neck.

All that remained to Glittershield was to swallow his enemy. First he rubbed his lips all over the body, from

71

the head to the tail, till it was slippery with slime. Then he opened his mouth very wide, with a huge snaky yawn, and face to face he began on Old Rattler. The ugly head was hard to manage, but, after much straining he clasped his jaws around it, and the venom trickled down his throat like some fiery sauce. Slowly head and neck and body disappeared, and the tail wriggled despairingly, for the tail of the snake folk can not die till sundown, and when it went at last the fifteen rattles and the button were keeping up an angry buzz. And all night long the King of Snakes, twice as big as he ought to be, lay gorged and motionless upon Old Rattler's rock.

And in the morning the little chipmunk ran out on a limb above him, pursed up his lips, and made all kinds of faces, as much as to say, 'I did all this, and the whole world was watching while I did it.'

THE COBRA

Ogden Nash

This creature fills its mouth with venum
And walks upon its duodenum
He who attempts to tease the cobra
Is soon a sadder he, and sobra.

WORMS AND THE WIND

Carl Sandburg

Worms would rather be worms.
Ask a worm and he says, 'Who knows what a worm knows?'
Worms go down and up and over and under.
Worms like tunnels.
When worms talk they talk about the worm world.
Worms like it in the dark.
Neither the sun nor the moon interests a worm.
Zigzag worms hate circle worms.
Curve worms never trust square worms.
Worms know what worms want.
Slide worms are suspicious of crawl worms.
One worm asks another, 'How does your belly drag today?'
The shape of a crooked worm satisfies a crooked worm.
A straight worm says, 'Why not be straight?'
Worms tired of crawling begin to slither.
Long worms slither farther than short worms.
Middle-sized worms say, 'It is nice to be neither long nor short
Old worms teach young worms to say, 'Don't be sorry for me
                        unless you have been a wor⟨
        and lived in worm places and read worm books.'
When worms go to war they dig in, come out and fight,
                        dig in again, come o⟨
        and fight again, dig in again, and so on.
Worms underground never hear the wind overground and
        sometimes they ask, 'What is this wind we hear of?'

Rats, Bats, and Mice

The Legend of the Pied Piper of Hamelin

Lucy Berman

In Hamelin, in Germany, a legendary plague of rats is said to have brought tragedy six hundred years ago. Hamelin was an old town, and rats were often seen there. They lived along the river and made nests in crumbling walls. Suddenly one awful spring, the population doubled: there were twice as many rats as there had ever been before. The numbers went on doubling until, sometime in summer, there were twenty rats per person, and the people lived in fear.

Not a single house in Hamelin was free of the invaders. The nests were everywhere: in the walls, and lofts and kitchens, under the stoves, behind the doors. Thousands lived down by the river, so that children could not swim there any more.

Daily the Mayor and his Corporation met to consider ways of dealing with the rats. Their meetings were interrupted by news of babies dead from rat-bites, of families without food.

'The rats are eating everything!' the Corporation cried. In the loft above their heads, the villains came and went. The pattering of busy feet threatened to drown out all discussion. Many ingenious traps were laid, but the only rats that were caught were elderly or sickly. An atmosphere of panic filled the Mayor's council chamber.

While they were reviewing the failure of yet another trap, a gentle knocking was heard at the door.

'Silence!' said the Mayor. 'Was that a rat scratching?'

The knocking came again. 'Come in,' the Mayor cried.

The door was opened quietly and a tall man entered the council chamber. He was unlike anyone in Hamelin. His blond hair fell below his shoulders. His eyes were blue and changeable. They seemed to be lit by a fire inside, glinting odd shades of green and gold. He was dressed in a flowing gown, half red, half yellow. At his waist, hung a slender wooden pipe, on which his right hand rested lovingly.

'Who are you,' said the Mayor, 'And what do you want?'

The stranger looked at the Mayor, who was fat and worried, and at the Corporation, who were fat and worried. 'I have been through the town,' he said, 'where they are thin and frightened. I have come to put things right. I am the Pied Piper. I go about playing tunes on my pipe and ridding people of their vermin. I can remove the rats from Hamelin.'

The Mayor pursed his lips. 'A fabrication,' he said.

The Piper's gaze flickered green. He produced a roll of papers from under his gown. 'Testimonials.' He passed them to the Mayor. 'The contents of these refer to the removal of ants and bats and lizards, newts, toads, salamanders, gophers, mice and moles.'

The Corporation peered over the Mayor's shoulders at the strange documents, all written in incomprehensible foreign tongues. 'We can't read these,' they protested.

'Well,' said the Piper, giving them a pale blue stare, 'you will have to believe me, then. Will you give me a thousand guilders when all the rats have gone?'

78

'We'll give you fifty thousand,' said the Mayor, 'if you can do it.'

The Pied Piper bowed and took his testimonials. He put them away under his gown and removed his pipe from the girdle at his waist. Then he stepped into the street and began to play.

An odd and unmelodious tune came bubbling from the pipe. In it were all the notes that rats use to call to one another: frantic squealings and high-pitched chirrups; and there were sounds that rats are never known to make, such as trills and gay, light-hearted whistles. The rats heard. Bounding along the alleys, scampering down the steps, they poured out of the houses to follow the Pied Piper. A column of rats, twenty feet broad, fell in behind him and overran the square.

He led them in procession through the town and to the river. There he waited for a moment, playing in a soothing manner while the old and sick and blind rats caught up with all the rest. When they were assembled, the Piper played a clarion note. The rats ran into the river, and every one was drowned.

People cried and hugged one another. They began to clear away rats' nests from cellars and lofts, singing as they worked. The Piper walked unnoticed to the council chamber, and went straight in.

'I'd like my thousand guilders, please,' he said.

The Mayor shook his head. 'Your methods were unorthodox and may have involved magic. I can't pay such sums to a travelling magician. The people would never hear of it.' (The Corporation nodded.) 'Take fifty guilders.'

The Piper's eyes glowed with a golden angry light. Again he stepped into the square and raised his wooden pipe. A sweet, laughing melody flooded through Hamelin. Before a dozen notes had sounded, the Piper

79

was surrounded by children. They followed him eagerly, more joining at every note.

'Come back,' the mothers cried. The children could not hear them, and the adults could not move. The music of the Pied Piper sent young people dancing and froze older people in their tracks.

The Piper led the children down toward the river. At the river's edge he shook his head and turned, and headed North.

'He's going up the mountain,' someone said, 'he must turn back. The children cannot climb that.'

The Piper stood for a moment at the foot of the mountain, playing in a soothing manner, while the lame and sickly children caught up with all the rest. Then he played a note of triumph. The mountain's face split open; a vast dark cave appeared. The Pied Piper entered, and the children—even those children who had always feared the dark—flocked behind him.

Ever more gaily, the Piper played. High, merry notes mocked the cries of fathers and mothers frozen like statues by the sound of his pipe. In despair they watched the last little blond head disappear into the mountain cave. The last bright face was gone from view. The parents of Hamelin stood and wept.

'We should have paid him,' groaned the Mayor. '*Fifty* thousand guilders. We *could* have paid him that much.'

The Piper's tune was fading out as he led the children into darkness. He blew a distant, curious whistle. The mountain shuddered and closed, covering the entrance to the cave. The people of Hamelin, freed from the Piper's spell, ran to the mountainside and searched and called. They pounded on the mountain, but there was no way in; not even a crack to show where the cave had been.

Disheartened, despairing, the people of Hamelin returned to their town where not a rat nor a child could be found. The Mayor put out an advertisement, offering all the money the Piper could want, if he would only bring the children home. But he never answered; he never came: he did not bring them home again. Hamelin town was lonely and bare, and it was always quiet there.

The Curse of Mouse Tower

Bernhardt J. Hurwood

About fifteen miles northwest of the city of Mainz there rises from the River Rhine a rock on which stands an ancient, forbidding tower, called *Mauseturm*, or Mouse Tower. According to local legend it is haunted by what may well be some of the most vengeful ghosts in all of Germany.

As the story goes, the tower was built around the 10th century by Hatto II, the Archbishop of Mainz, who used it as a tollhouse. The bishop was not a kindly man and he imposed harsh taxes and heavy tolls throughout the district, thereby reducing the peasants to a state of abject poverty. One year, as a result of storms and droughts a severe famine made matters worse.

Although the crops had been devastated, Hatto owned a number of storehouses in which ample grain had been stocked during the previous seasons when nature had been kind to the land and its people. Instead of distributing it to the needy, or even selling it to those who could afford to pay a lower price, he offered it only at a high price to those with ready cash. Needless to say, there were fewer of these people each day. Finally, in desperation, a delegation representing the majority who were on the verge of starvation, came to Hatto and begged him to lower the price to a range that they could afford. But he refused and turned them away.

Driven by their hunger to persist they returned and petitioned him again, begging him to relent and to save them from starvation. This time he appeared to undergo a change of heart. He listened and finally told them that if they went to a certain barn outside the town of Bingen across from the *Mauseturm*, each person could have as much grain as he could carry home by himself. With gratitude and relief, the peasants flocked to the barn with empty sacks, kegs, anything they could find to fill with grain. But once they got inside they were startled to find themselves locked in. Confusion gave way to terror when the acrid smell of smoke struck their nostrils, for it was then that the realization struck that they had been betrayed, and that Hatto's henchmen had deliberately set the barn on fire.

As the flames crackled and roared amidst the frenzied shrieks and the billowing smoke, a single choking woman managed to find her way to a window where she shrieked a curse at the cruel bishop that all outside could hear.

'May your sufferings exceed ours by a thousandfold!' she cried. 'May the rats from the river and the fields devour the living flesh from your bones before you die, and may your miserable soul be shackled to your accursed tower for as long as it stands!'

Hatto scoffed at the curse when he was told of it, for he had not even bothered to come and witness the slaughter of his innocent victims. After one of his customary sumptuous meals, he retired for the night. He was awakened in the middle of the night by a sound that he had never heard before, and by the time he found out what it was there was no escape. Swarms of rats had invaded his palace, huge, ferocious rats, with beady bright eyes and gleaming sharp teeth. The sound of tiny claws pattering on stone multiplied by tens of thousands was enough to drive a man insane, and the horrible squeaking and squealing and gnashing of teeth was beyond description. Fleeing in terror from room to room as the frenzied horde of hungry rats pursued him, Hatto finally managed to get out of the palace.

The tower! It was his only hope of refuge. Running as fast as he could to the banks of the Rhine, he scrambled into a boat and rowed to the rock. Then lighting a candle inside the tower, he climbed to its uppermost room, where he collapsed in a chair panting with exhaustion and terror. Soon he fell asleep, but after a while, how long he did not know, he was awakened again. The candle had long since burned out and he was surrounded by darkness. The wind was blowing, moaning, and wailing like a thousand lost souls. But above it there were other sounds—*squeaking and squealing, pattering of feet and gnashing of teeth!*

The rats had come!

This time there was no escape. Dropping to his knees, Hatto began to pray, but his prayers were not answered. When the thousands of furry horrors swarmed over him his screams were drowned by the gnawing, the tearing, the squealing, and the grinding. And by the time they had finished, there was nothing left of him but a pile of white bones. But it was not quite the end of Hatto, for even today, his tortured phantom rushes about the gloomy corridors of Mouse Tower, shrieking and moaning, wailing and begging for mercy, and everyone who knows the story is convinced that so will it be with the evil man's ghost as long as a single stone of Mouse Tower remains.

The Mouse

Henry Williamson

A dark thing, wretched and lowly, dragged itself among
the frozen elm-leaves and the hardening mud. It knew
by smell that if it could reach the wall in front, it would
be safe. Its nose, nearly hidden by a ruby crust of blood,
told that others of its kind had recently passed among
the leaves and the mud on the way to the hole in the old
cob wall. The lowly thing crept laboriously, because it
was weak and its hind legs were bitten.

A weasel had been tracking the field mouse in a garden, and had caught it, biting its legs as it rustled desperately through a chink in the wall. The mouse had
screamed, and the white apparition on the top of the wall
bent a head downwards and detected with black round
eyes the movement below.

Fortunately for the mouse—it was but chance, for
nothing protected the wee parcel of life in the browny-
red coat—the apparition gazed on the side it was not,
thus seeing the weasel. It would have been quite as
convenient for the barn owl to turn his head, without
moving his body, and to peer down his back; indeed, a
complete swivelling of the head was natural and easy to
the bird with the fixed eyes. Chance was that it saw the
moving weasel, that it slipped noiselessly down the wall

and gripped the body with a taloned foot. The weasel chattered, and fixed its teeth in the foot just before the talons, instantly puncturing hair, skin and ribs, pierced the hunter's heart, and life sank away.

The scent of the creature dismayed the owl, who screeched, dropped it dying into a cabbage pulped by rain and bored by caterpillars, and flew up into the elms. The field mouse, which had gone into the garden in order to find food, lay quivering. Its beady eyes were wide with fear, its legs ached, its long ears drooped.

Some time later it stirred, and lifted its ears. Its smell, usually so keen and helpful, was dulled; it had to breathe through its mouth. It crawled forward, pausing often lest the terror return. It dragged itself over frozen mud craters and across brittle ice, coming at last to the wall. One desire the mouse had, to creep into its hole and lie still. Its tail was cold and stiffening, it could see but indistinctly; it must reach the hole where there would be no terror, no pain in its legs, and no noise to make its heart close in its throat.

At last the sanctuary was reached, and with stronger steps the mouse disappeared within, safe and so happy that it squeaked a welcome. Finding a dry nook it curled up, wrapped its head in its paws, and slept.

All the long January night the mouse was curled in the dusty corner. Quick patterings and dull thumpings passed near, but it did not wake. Greenish circles came with the patterings, and went out as the rats disappeared round the corner. Once the sleeper leapt sideways, bumping its head, and trembling at the grunts that seemed to envelop it. But the doe-rat had no young, so the mouse was not bitten.

Later a grey light came into the tunnel, and the mouse was awake, feeling hungry, and remembering nothing of the night's horror. It limped along in the dust till it came to an opening bigger than its body. A beam of light poured through this crack in the cottage wall and showed an animal hunched in a corner. The thing never moved, but remained as though it were eating something. No scent came from it, and the mouse crept nearer.

The thing remained in the same position, looking like a bullying rat; it had a tail, but no hair was on it: it had ears, but stiff and brittle: it had paws and legs and body, a head, but all furless, dried and inanimate. Although it appeared to hold food in its paws, there was no food there; while the teeth were long, yellow, and projecting in two curls—one upwards over its snout and the other downwards under its chin. The mouse trembled, wrinkled its nose, and bolted as fast as a broken hindfoot would permit.

It returned to the nook, and dozed, pain preventing sleep. It was startled by thunderous noises. To its surprise, this new terror was not greeted by the silence and stillness of all things, but by squeaks, thumpings, and swift patterings in the tunnel. The mouse knew that the thunder was therefore undirected to itself, and there being no hostile smell, it emerged and followed the rats.

Past the motionless object made grey and fearsome by the light it limped, passing many turnings, side-tunnels, and twistings. After a long and gradual descent it came to a round hole very white beyond. With caution the mouse approached the glare of day, trying to smell through the clotted blood on its nose. Immense noises came to the hole, but as large rats were running over the floor beyond there seemed no danger; and it must get to some unmolested place; why, it knew not, but it must.

The first thunderous noises had been made by an old man getting out of bed, and dressing. His dressing did not take long, for all he had to do was to insert his swollen feet into a pair of botched boots. When this was done he clumped away from the bed, an affair of rusty iron, single mouldy blanket, a dozen corn sacks, and a bag of straw. On the dry board littered with plaster and dust his boots shuffled and clumped, for the old man was bent nearly double by rheumatism. With the help of a stick grasped in a root-like hand he shuffled down the wooden stairs and entered the living room.

On the lime-ash floor his boots clanked, and hardly had he opened the door of the bodley—as the Devon hamlet folk called the kitchen range—to get his loaf and cheese, when three rats emerged from a hole, ran up the table leg, and waited among the grease stains near the one chair. George Miles put the bread and cheese on the table, drew up the chair with difficulty, and wheezily sat down. Meanwhile other rats had scampered out of the hole, and were climbing up his trousers, perching on his shoulders, his head; some, with the familiarity of a long friendship, began to wash their faces while waiting.

'Ullo midears,' croaked the ancient, 'my li'l boys come to see granfer, hey! Bide awhile, midears, an' granfer wull give ee zum brakfust.'

A palsied hand was inserted into a coat pocket, and a knife taken out. After many attempts to open the single blade he succeeded, and hacked a slice off the loaf, cutting it into pieces which he distributed among the scrambling rats. They seized them, squatted on hind-legs, and little noises of nibbling mingled with the harsh breathing of the old man. When all had been fed he cut himself a slice and then began his own meal; with hard gums he muched the bread and cheese, regarding the rats as he ate and sometimes stroking one.

Then his misty eyes saw a mouse wandering feebly over the floor. Although he was nearly blind, the old stonecracker could see that the mouse was hurt. Since early youth he had been accustomed to sit by the roadside, and always he had loved to watch the wild creatures of the hedges and ditches. Now he spoke to the hurt mouse, who crept nearer to him without any fear. He picked it up in his hand and watched it crouching there. Its bright beady eyes looked at him—small crawling rodent and ancient lonely man, living breathing things.

'Gordarn if ee bant a bootiful l'il boy,' the ancient chuckled, 'Don't reckons ah've zeen ee afore, maister. Ah'll be dalled if ee bant hungrisome, too. Well mi-boy, you'm welcome. Li'l Jearge ah'll call ee, because my name be Jearge. Gordarn, fancy a wild un coming to see Granfer Jearge.'

For an hour the old man sat there with Li'l Jearge in his palm, telling him how pretty a mouse he was and how his l'il boy must stop along of him. Li'l Jearge ate some crumbs, then ceased eating because of sudden pain. In the horny palm of its patron's hand it crouched, its head leaning to one side, waiting.

3

Ponderous steps rang on the cobbles outside, and George Miles was glad that Uncle Joe was out and about. The footsteps drew up outside the door, and a voice said it was gude weather fur the time o' year. George Miles croaked for the door to be opened, and after some fumbling at

89

the latch, the room became lighter, and all the rats were fled into their ancestral highways of the yard-thick cob wall, passing the mummified rat that had remained there while on the rafters above the single bedroom over a hundred broods of owlets had been raised; one brood being raised in a summer.

'Aiy, it be gude weather fur the time o' year, Granfer Jearge,' said Uncle Joe, slowly. He called the other Granfer with the respect that all Devon men pay to age. Uncle Joe was seventy-seven, and that was not so old; whereas Granfer was nearly ninety, a very great age.

Uncle Joe wore a check cap given him by his reverence the parson ten years ago, only he wore the peak over his ear, pointing to the sky, so that it no longer appeared to be a cap; rather did it resemble a piece of rag thrown by someone out of a window and coming to rest on his white head as he passed under it. His face was long and pale, with a clipped beard; his eyes were like the blue petals of a flower under thawing ice.

'Aiy, it be zeasonable weather, sure-nuff,' mused Uncle Joe. 'I be going to look at my seedling tetties. Aiy. Aiy. Well, I be going. Aiy.'

He took nearly a minute to announce and corroborate this statement, said 'Aiy' once again, mentioned that if the weather did not change it would remain as it was, confirmed the prophecy with a further aiy, and shuffled away to his potatoes.

All the while Granfer Jearge, who lived on an Old Age Pension, whose wife was dead, whose children and grandchildren and great-grandchildren were away in furrin parts—some reckoned to be as far away as London—all the while Old Jearge nursed the mouse. It was then, as he sat musing, that Li'l Jearge gave birth to her first litter of six tinies.

Granfer Jearge borrowed from Uncle Joe a cardboard

box, and made a home for Li'l Jearge and her tinies. Even such a thing as a cardboard box had to be begged, because in his own cottage Granfer Jearge had no furniture save a chair with mildewed legs, a yellow candle stuck in a champagne bottle with tarnished gold-foil, the table, a battered bucket, and a clock. Jearge was proud of the bottle, which the old squire returning from a shoot in a dogcart had jocularly thrown at him (this was just before the failure to make his iron-mining pay, and his death from alcoholic poisoning. That had occurred twenty years ago; even so, Jearge thought of it as happening last year, or yesterday).

The clock was, in his senile estimation, a most valuable one, and worth quite ten shillings. So valuable did the old man consider it that he never wound it up, in order to save wear and tear of the works. These articles, with a holy picture of an ill-shaped woman offering fruit to what looked like a waxen tailor's dummy, comprised all his furniture. *Adam and Eve before the Fall* hung awry, and a spider had found it convenient to attach a net to it. Some day, Granfer told Uncle Joe, he would hold an auction and sell the picture and the clock, when times were bad, as they would be if they stopped his pension.

Several times every day the retired railway porter commented on the weather, standing in the open doorway with his cap-peak pointing to the sky where eventually he would go. One afternoon was so warm that Granfer Jearge pottered about his garden, and found a dead weasel in one of the cabbages. The location of the animal caused him to mutter many words to himself. Then Uncle Joe plodded by, and as usual, stopped.

'What do ee think I've found, Joo, in a cabbage?'

'What be ut?'

'A li'l dead fitchey.'

'Have un been eating your cabbage, Granfer Jearge?'

'Noomye. Fitcheys eat mice and such things.'

'Aiy. That be strange. Aiy. I do hear Bill Thorn be going to kill ees pig zoon. Aiy.'

'Once 'a zeed a fitchey run away from a znake.'

'Aiy. He do reckon the pig to vetch eighteen score. Aiy.'

'One of them master girt znakes down by the mines, it were, zactly.'

'They do zay pigsment wull a-come down tuppence zoon.'

'Aiy.'

'Aiy aiy.'

Granfer Jearge slung the weasel over the wall, and went indoors. Later a small boy from a near cottage came and stared at him. The door remained open, for the sun was warm.

'Ullo, miboy!' greeted the ancient.

'Granfer Jar,' murmured the child. Mud and jam were blended on his face and hands; he had reflective brown eyes and golden curls.

'Come urr, midear,' persuaded the ancient, 'look what Granfer hev got.'

He showed Ernie (for that was the name of the little tacker) the box, and Li'l Jearge within, content with her six tinies. Their eyes were now open, and so was the mouth of Ernie.

'Whatsat?' he inquired at last.

'Li'l Jearge, midear.'

'It be yours, bant it? It bant mine, be it? Watsat?'

'Li'l mousie, midear.'

'Be it yours?'

'Aiy.'

'It bant mine, be it? It be yours, bant it? Where you get un to?'

'Her coomed in yurr.'

93

'Her did?'

'Aiy.'

'It be yours, bant it? It bant mine, be it?'

The monotonous child Ernie would probably have continued to emphasise his four-year-old knowledge of the law of *meum et tuum* till his mother shrilled for his return, had not Uncle Joe, who had been staring steadily at the sky, clumped along and interrupted.

'I didn't tell ee, did I, bout my seedling tetties? I reckon them to be growing too fast. Aiy.'

He stared at Granfer Jearge uneasily.

'Aiy,' he repeated.

4

The same uneasiness was shown on the following day, as though Uncle Joe knew something that Granfer Jearge did not. For Uncle Joe had heard that Farmer Goldsworthy intended to turn out the ancient, because his rent was two years overdue; and to do this Farmer Goldsworthy, so said rumour, had made application to the Union Guardians, so that Granfer Jearge should be put in 'the Grubber', or Workhouse.

And Granfer Jearge knew nothing of this, for everyone was afraid to tell him.

At the Nightcrow Inn, Brownie, a mason's mate with a black moustache and one gentle brown eye, a tenderhearted father of many children, lamented the decision of the Union Guardians that Granfer Jearge was an incapable.

'He wull veel it turrible, I do reckon.' His voice had a natural rise and fall in speaking that gave the listeners a mournful sympathy for Granfer. 'He'm having lived in the parish fur so long, and maaked up the roads roundabout.'

When Farmer Goldsworthy took away Granfer Jearge's clock as part payment of the rent there was more talk in the village. The ancient appeared in the village street, tapping along with his stick and bent double, a corrugated chimney-hat without a top to it stuck on his head.

'He cried to lose ees clock,' reported Brownie, 'and did talk of going to get th' schoolmaster to write a letter on it to the Queen, darn me! Ho-ho-ho-ho-ho-ho! But it bant no laughing episode, noomye! It were his vather's afore him, and went most bootiful, it did, most loud-ticking clock in th' parish. Reckon poor old Jearge's heart wull be broke when he'm in thiccy Grubber.'

The morning when the relieving officer came to warn him to prepare to move out, Granfer Jearge was thinking about eating, as a great treat, the one cabbage remaining. The news made him sit down, and for two hours he did not stir. Uncle Joe came and moped at the door, but all Jearge could say was 'hey?'

When he was young, George Miles had been by turn crowstarver, carter's lad, kitchen boy, ploughboy, and eventually stonecracker. At the age of twenty-three he had fallen in love with a maid, and married. Till he was seventy, he never made more than eleven shillings a week, and to earn that he worked six days a week from early morn till after sunset. But he had been happy in his way, for he had been able to pay all his small debts, and to have a glass of ale when he wanted it. Two of his four children he had buried in the churchyard, and over the green mounds the rooks cawed in their colony. His two sons went off somewhere, and they may have died; his grandchildren never came to see him: he owned no property.

When his wife died Granfer Jearge continued to live on in the cottage until all emotion had run from his withered heart, as the dust spills from the core of a pollard oak whose last leaves have fallen from it. But as an old tree can shelter much life—nuthatches, titmice, woodlice, an owl—so Granfer Jearge, reft of bud, leaf and fruit, made friends with the despised things of the earth.

The rats were affectionate animals, and showed, in miniature, a dog-like attitude towards him. They came when he called them, they played on the table with one another, they paused at a strange noise outside and bared their teeth as a dog will. Granfer Jearge delighted to see them washing, and he never ceased to marvel at their clean habits. They combed their whiskers, groomed themselves with paw and tongue, washed their faces after each meal, and seldom quarrelled.

Granfer was content, believing that until the Dear Lord called him he would live at honest peace with everything—and then came the officer with his dread news, like a woodman to fell the pollard oak. Granfer wheezed his woe to Li'l Jearge. He were going into the Grubber. It were a turrible disgrace. Man and boy he had paid his way, and now to end in the Grubber. His brain repeated dully the same thoughts: they were going to put him in the Grubber, they were. For this he had toiled and toiled at stone-cracking, bringing up children, tending his pig and tettie-garden through all the years; he had never spent his money at the Inn, as some had; he had paid Varmer the rent reg'lar since he were wed except a bit recently—and now they were taking him away to the Grubber.

That night he made a bit of a fire, and lit the candle that he had been saving up for the future. Before the smoulder of furze-roots and driftwood he sat trembling, mouth open, with split blue lip fallen, staring with worn-out eyes at the rusted bodley. No one had baked in the

96

oven for a dozen years; no hymn had been sung since Lou his wife had died; and now who would tend his mouse? He prayed the Dear Lord would be good, and take him that night to Lou up above the sky.

But in the morning Hope came to him. He would take Li'l Jearge with him into the Grubber!

5

The carrier came to the door, and asked if Granfer were ready.

'Aiy.'

In a sack he carried his scanty wardrobe, and the chimney-pot hat was on his head.

'What be these, Granfer?' abruptly asked the carrier, pointing to the pile of sacks and the mouldy blanket.

'Thaccy be my proberty.'

'Well, you won't want they things in Barum, noomye! Better be burnt, I reckon. And what's the bottle for?'

'That be a vall-uable bottle, midear, becass t'old zquire drowed un at me long ago.'

'Aw, you be too old-fashioned, midear,' replied the carrier. 'Come along now, I be a busy man these days. You must look out for yourself these days, for no one else will help 'ee, you knows that, don't ee, Granfer?'

So from the cottage in which he had lived for nearly a century, to which he had taken a comely maid to wife, and reared his children, departed George Miles, stone-cracker, with his picture, his bottle, and the box containing Li'l Jearge and her tinies. Slowly he dragged himself among the damp elm-leaves and the mud, tapping with his stick, his body curved like a sickle. He never turned to take a last glance at the thatched cottage, or the garden, or Uncle Joe watching silently while his cap-peak pointed to heaven. Housewives came to cottage doors and stared—Granfer Jearge were going into the Grubber, he were. Poor chap, some whispered, he wouldn't last long now.

But Granfer Jearge made no moan or spoke no word of any kind. Slower and slower his feet lagged. When he was hoisted up on the jingle-cart Ernie came by and said in his sweet, winsome voice:

'You be gwin away, Granfer Jearge? I ban't be gwin away, be I? Tis you be gwin. It bant me, be ut?'

But Granfer on the seat made no sign that he had heard the voice of his dear little friend Ernie. His eyes were fixed with an unseeing stare, his mouth was open. Suddenly Ernie cried:

'Look, there ut be! Granfer's got that one! I ain't got that one! It be Granfer got that one!'

Granfer Jearge sat still, leaning on his stick. The box in his pocket had opened, and Li'l Jearge, tired of her tinies for a while, had climbed to his shoulder. The carrier knocked it off with a sharp and accurate blow of his hand, and Li'l Jearge fell on the road below. It was dazed, and while it hesitated a housewife put her foot on it, crushing out all life. Ernie began to cry, his small heart touched with pity.

One of the young mice showed itself above his pocket, and the carrier remarked that Granfer appeared to be a nest of vermin, poor old fellow. The lookers-on agreed that it was time for someone to take care of him. By the wall a cat was crouching, a thin black creature with high ears, existing on and allowed to exist because of rats, and as the small mice were shaken out of the box it bounded forward and ate all except one, a sharp little fellow, who nipped into a hole under a stone.

'Now us'll be off, Granfer,' called genially the carrier. 'A bootiful day for a drive, and a bowl of hot zoup fur ee at Barum.'

Uncle Joe scraped over the road, just to bid him a safe journey.

'Well, good-bye, Granfer Jearge,' his voice quavered. 'It wull keep fine, I reckon. My zeedling tetties by cuming on terrible fast. Aiy they be.'

He paused, and spat; then stared at his old neighbour. 'What, be feeling bad, Granfer?'

Now they were all looking at him. 'My dear soul—' cried Uncle Joe, and the pipe dropped from his mouth.

Shortly afterwards Granfer Jearge was back in the cottage, and lying on the table, unmoving, like a disused sickle. Uncle Joe was trembling and muttering in his own house, the door shut fast. Ernie too was indoors and asking questions of his mother, who in a low voice was rapidly speaking to three neighbours.

A noise under the stairs, the tip-tap of claws on stone, a squeak, and the rats were out of their wall castle, running up the table legs for food. On the accustomed figure they perched, combing their whiskers. An old doe rose on her hind legs, sniffing. Suddenly all were still.

Then they fled from the figure, and gathered together at the end of the table in a group, as though they were discussing something. They perched on their hind legs, and sniffed. It was very quiet in the cottage. First one, then another, ran down the table leg, swiftly across the floor, and into the tunnel, passing the brown mummy with its curled teeth and hairless tail crouched in still attitude on the dust.

The Vampire Bats

William Beebe

The bats were with us from first to last. We exterminated one colony which spent its inverted days clustered over the centre of our supply chamber, but others came immediately and disputed the ownership of the dark room. Little chaps with great ears and nose-tissue of sensitive skin, spent the night beneath my shelves and chairs, and even my cot. They hunted at dusk and again at dawn, slept in my room and vanished in the day. Even for bats they were ferocious, and whenever I caught one in a butterfly-net, he went into paroxysms of rage, squealing in angry passion, striving to bite my hand and, failing that, chewing vainly on his own long fingers and arms. Their teeth were wonderfully intricate and seemed adapted for some very special diet, although beetles seemed to satisfy those which I caught. For once, the systematist had labelled them opportunely, and we never called them anything but *Furipterus horrens*.

In the evening, great bats as large as small herons swept down the long front gallery where we worked, gleaning as they went; but the vampires were long in coming, and for months we neither saw nor heard of one. Then they attacked our servants, and we took heart, and night after night exposed our toes, as conventionally accepted vampire-bait. When at last they found that the colour of our skins was no criterion of dilution of blood, they came in crowds. For three nights they swept about us with hardly a whisper of wings, and accepted either toe or elbow or finger, or all three, and the cots and floor in the morning looked like an emergency hospital behind an active front. In spite of every attempt at keeping awake, we dropped off to sleep before the bats had begun, and did not waken until they left. We ascertained, however, that there was no truth in the belief that they hovered or kept fanning with their wings. Instead, they settled on the person with an appreciable flop and then crawled to the desired spot.

One night I made a special effort and, with bared arm, prepared for a long vigil. In a few minutes bats began to fan my face, the wings almost brushing, but never quite touching my skin. I could distinguish the difference between the smaller and the larger, the latter having a deeper swish, deeper and longer drawn-out. Their voices were so high and shrill that the singing of the jungle crickets seemed almost contralto in comparison. Finally, I began to feel myself the focus of one or more of these winged weasels. The swishes became more frequent, the returnings almost doubling on their track. Now and then a small body touched the sheet for an instant, and then, with a soft little tap, a vampire alighted on my chest. I was half sitting up, yet I could not see him, for I had found that the least hint of light ended any possibility of a visit. I breathed as quietly as I could, and made sure that both hands were clear. For a long time there was no movement, and the renewed swishes made me suspect that the bat had again taken flight. Not until I felt a tickling on my wrist did I know that my visitor had shifted and, unerringly, was making for the arm which I had exposed. Slowly it crept forward, but I hardly felt the pushing of the feet and pulling of the thumbs as it crawled along. If I had been asleep, I should not have awakened. It continued up my forearm and came to rest at my elbow. Here another long period of rest, and then several short, quick shifts of body. With my whole attention concentrated on my elbow, I began to imagine various sensations as my mind pictured the long, lancet tooth sinking deep into the skin, and the blood pumping up. I even began to feel the hot rush of my vital fluid over my arm, and then found that I had dozed for a moment and that all my sensations were imaginary. But soon a gentle tickling became apparent, and, in spite of putting this out of my mind and with increasing doubts as to the bat being still there, the tickling continued. It changed to a tingling, rather pleasant than otherwise, like the first stage of having one's hand asleep.

It really seemed as if this were the critical time. Somehow or other the vampire was at work with no pain or even inconvenience to me, and now was the moment to seize him, call for a lantern, and solve his supersurgical skill, the exact method of this vespertilial anaesthetist. Slowly, very slowly, I lifted the other hand, always thinking of my elbow, so that I might keep all the muscles relaxed. Very slowly it approached, and with as swift a motion as I could achieve, I grasped at the vampire. I felt a touch of fur and I gripped a struggling, skinny wing; there came a single nip of teeth, and the wing-tip slipped through my fingers. I could detect no trace of blood by feeling, so turned over and went to sleep. In the morning I found a tiny scratch, with the skin barely broken; and, heartily disappointed, I realized that my tickling and tingling had been the preliminary symptoms of the operation.

RATS

Joan Beadon

Classed now as pests,
Outcasts, oppressed;
Shot, trapped, poisoned, worried,
Pressed flat on summer roads;
Shabby synonyms of evil, yes,
But a nuisance only,
Not to be taken seriously
(Except by hysterical women,
Farmers and public health officials,
Themselves not to be taken seriously);
The rats hide in stacks and ships
And by the side of dark canals and refuse tips;
From cats and dogs and men with sticks
They cower
And bide their certain hour.

They fall in thousands, those of them
Foolish enough to feed upon our bait.
The rest, the wise ones, breed and wait,
Watching the wheel turn, their action call.

When hate and fate and fall-out
Have done their work, their worst,
And men that survive once more
Lurk in caves along the barren shore,
The rats will emerge from some deep tomb,
Singly at first and without sound,
And then by two and ten and squeaking score,
Fifties and hundreds and still hundreds more,
To surge like lava over the littered ground,
Destroy all human wisdom and consume

All science, all art and beauty we have known,
Burn cloth from flesh and flesh from chiselled bone
Till 'Rat' is all that is.

Foreknowing this, they yet evince
No pride, take no offence
At present insult, are content
To watch us engineer our going hence—
As we watched lordly saurians uncounted centuries since.

saurians: dinosaurs

BATS

Randall Jarrell

A bat is born
Naked and blind and pale.
His mother makes a pocket of her tail
And catches him. He clings to her long fur
By his thumbs and toes and teeth.
And then the mother dances through the night
Doubling and looping, soaring, somersaulting—
Her baby hangs on underneath.
All night, in happiness, she hunts and flies.
Her high sharp cries
Like shining needlepoints of sound
Go out into the night and, echoing back,
Tell her what they have touched.
She hears how far it is, how big it is,
Which way it's going:
She lives by hearing.
The mother eats the moths and gnats she catches

In full flight; in full flight
The mother drinks the water of the pond
She skims across. Her baby hangs on tight.
Her baby drinks the milk she makes him
In moonlight or starlight, in mid-air.
Their single shadow, printed on the moon
Or fluttering across the stars,
Whirls on all night; at daybreak
The tired mother flaps home to her rafter.
The others all are there.
They hang themselves up by their toes,
They wrap themselves in their brown wings.
Bunched upside-down, they sleep in air.
Their sharp ears, their sharp teeth, their quick
        sharp faces
Are dull and slow and mild.
All the bright day, as the mother sleeps,
She folds her wings about her sleeping child.

THE MOUSE'S TAIL

Lewis Carroll

They sat down again in a ring, and begged the Mouse to
tell them something.

'You promised to tell me your history, you know,' said
Alice, 'and why it is you hate—C and D,' she added in a
whisper, half afraid that it would be offended again.

'Mine is a long and sad tale!' said the Mouse, turning
to Alice and sighing.

'It *is* a long tail, certainly,' said Alice, looking down
with wonder at the Mouse's tail; 'but why do you call it

sad?' And she kept on puzzling about it while the Mouse
was speaking, so that her idea of the tale was something
like this:

'Fury said to a
mouse, That he
met in the
house,
"Let us
both go to
law: *I* will
prosecute
you. Come,
I'll take no
denial; We
must have a
trial: For
really this
morning I've
nothing
to do."
Said the
mouse to the
cur, "Such
a trial,
dear Sir,
With
no jury
or judge,
would be
wasting
our
breath."
"I'll be
a judge, I'll
be jury,"
said
cunning
old Fury:
"I'll
try the
whole
cause
and
condemn
you
to
death."'

Scorpions
and Ants

The Scorpion

Richard Henwood

The Scorpion is zoologically classified as a member of the *Arachnida*, a group comprising spiders, scorpions, and mites.

In its general appearance the Scorpion resembles a miniature lobster, the most prominent features being a pair of large claws or pincers, and a tail which arches backwards over its body. At the tip of this tail is housed a sting the pain of which is as exquisite as it is near fatal. Measuring between two to eight inches in length the Scorpion is to be found in tropical and warm temperate zones, both north and south of the equator, where it secretes itself beneath shady rock-ledges or stones, inside a bed or boot perhaps as many an unsuspecting soul has discovered to his cost.

Little by way of legend attaches specifically to this

charming little fellow whose sting is out of all proportion to his size. To the ancients, who believed that the stars and the planets influenced both men and events on earth, the Scorpion was of interest in that it symbolised the forces and various distinguishing features of that part of the heavens dominated by the constellation to which it has given its name—Scorpio, or more generally speaking, the eighth sign of the Zodiac. And within this constellation the star Antares has become known as 'the Scorpion's Heart'. The ancients represented the eighth sign of the Zodiac thus ♏, the symbol loosely depicting the legs and tail of the Scorpion, and for many of them it was a sign of evil influence, the Mayas calling it the 'Sign of the death-god'. To the early civilizations of the middle-east, however, the sign of Scorpio was represented by a centaur—half man, half scorpion. In time the man was replaced by an Eagle, and the scorpion—a Serpent. In the eyes of the magicians and prophets of those times the centaur represented man's two-fold nature—the Eagle symbolising his possibility for spiritual development, and the Serpent his lower nature, his material state.

With the death in 1727 of Sir Isaac Newton, to whom we owe the Law of Universal Gravitation, and with the birth of pure scientific method the idea that the heavens, the sun and orbiting planets which traversed them, could affect events on earth fell into disrepute. The study of planetary influences, known as *astrology*, became bracketed with other traditional kinds of superstition such as magic, witchcraft and fortune-telling for which the penalty, if practised, was death. In its place the new science of *astronomy* flourished.

But in recent years there has come about a revival of interest in the study of astrology associated possibly with the onset of the so-called 'Age of Aquarius' and the gradual decline of organised religion as we have known it for many centuries. And on the assumption that each of the twelve Zodiacal signs, or 'houses' as they are sometimes referred to, acts as 'host' to the sun for roughly one month of the year, and that approximately one-twelfth of humanity can be said to have been born in any one month, we may examine the influences which supposedly affect a person born between the 23rd of October and the 21st of November when the sun is traversing the Sign of Scorpio, the eighth house of the Zodiac.

*   *   *

Study the eyes of a Scorpio friend, relative, or casual acquaintance: note their blackness and emotional intensity, the silent, cautious watchfulness, their magnetic quality—and remember the Scorpion lurking beneath that slab of rock, the suppressed power within its tail awaiting release. Not that one should press the likeness too far for the fathomless reservoir of energy which Scorpio subjects seem to possess, can be used for good or ill, just as Ares, god of War in Greek mythology, who rules this sign, was not without his good points. Properly directed this Martian energy can be the means of attaining great heights of endeavour comparable with the Eagle who soars aloft and surveys the ground beneath, before plummeting down to seize his unsuspecting quarry.

For the individual born under the sign of Scorpio the 'quarry' or goal is to know the underlying nature of things: the cause behind the effect; the secrets that people withold from all but him. The roots of a problem he lays bare with the delicate precision of a surgeon's knife—nothing remaining hidden from his perceptive, probing mind, for above all the Scorpio native lives for truth, in pursuit of which he is relentless.

He who is born under the sign of Scorpio is basically a creature of extremes, though such tendencies may be moderated by the influences of other planets. In high, good humour the Scorpio subject will be the 'life and soul of the party'; but when unhappy or depressed his ill-spirits will drag down those of all around him. Ordinarily, he exhibits high standards in such qualities as courtesy, generosity, loyalty, and sympathy; but when angered his fury knows no bounds: he becomes headstrong, selfish, and prone to making hurtful, cutting remarks. As a friend he will prove loyal and courageous; as an enemy he is best avoided.

For all the general strength of character which distinguishes the Scorpio-born, he is not without the sensitivity which befits a sign associated with the natural *element* of water. And it is through his emotions, symbolically represented by this element, that he can best be influenced.

Amongst their number Scorpios include great healers, surgeons, psychologists and psychiatrists, lawyers, inventors, detectives, research-workers, soldiers, and undertakers. They have a natural liking for those born under the Zodiacal influence of Pisces, Cancer, Taurus, Virgo and Capricorn.

Scorpio is associated with the number 9; the day Tuesday; the colour red; the gemstone topaz; the metal iron; and such plants as thistles, cactus, onions, garlic, horseradish, leeks, mustard, watercress, nettles, rhubarb, tobacco, hawthorn, heather, chives, boxwood, oak, sandalwood, hemlock and tamrack. The strongest sense of the Scorpio-born is taste.

Wilhelmina

Gerald Durrell

Most people, when they learn for the first time that I collect wild animals for zoos, ask the same series of questions in the same order. First they ask if it is dangerous, to which the answer is no, it is not, providing you do not make any silly mistakes. Then they ask how I catch the animals—a more difficult question to answer, for there are many hundreds of ways of capturing wild animals: sometimes you have no set method, but have to improvise something on the spur of the moment. Their third question is, invariably: don't you become attached to your animals and find it difficult to part with them at the end of an expedition? The answer is, of course, that you do, and sometimes parting with a creature you have kept for eight months can be a heartbreaking process.

Occasionally you even find yourself getting attached to the strangest of beasts, some weird creature you would never in the normal way have thought you could like. One such beast as this, I remember, was Wilhelmina.

Wilhelmina was a whip-scorpion, and if anyone had told me that the day would come when I would feel even the remotest trace of affection for a whip-scorpion I would never have believed them. Of all the creatures on the face of this earth the whip-scorpion is one of the least prepossessing. To those who do not adore spiders (and I am one of those people) the whip-scorpion is a form of living nightmare. It resembles a spider with a body the size of a walnut that has been run over by a steamroller and flattened to a wafer-thin flake. To this flake are attached what appear to be an immense number of long, fine and crooked legs which spread out to the size of a soup-plate. To cap it all, on the front (if such a creature can be said to have a front), are two enormously long slender legs like whips, about twelve inches long in a robust specimen. It possesses the ability to skim about at incredible speed and with apparently no effort —up, down or sideways—and to squeeze its revolting body into a crack that would scarcely accommodate a piece of tissue-paper.

That is a whip-scorpion, and to anyone who distrusts spiders it is the personification of the devil. Fortunately they are harmless, unless you happen to have a weak heart.

I made my first acquaintance with Wilhelmina's family when I was on a collecting trip to the tropical forest of West Africa. For many different reasons, hunting in these forests is always difficult. To begin with, the trees are enormous, some as much as a hundred and fifty feet high, with trunks as fat as a factory chimney. Their head foliage is thick, luxuriant and twined with creepers and the branches are decorated with various parasitic plants like a curious hanging garden. All this may be eighty or a hundred feet above the forest floor, and the only way to reach it is to climb a trunk as smooth as a plank which has not a single branch for the first seventy feet of its length. This, the top layer of the forest, is by far the most thickly populated, for in the comparative safety of the tree-tops live a host of creatures which rarely, if ever, descends to ground-level. Setting traps in the forest canopy is a difficult and tedious operation. It may take the whole morning to find a way up a tree, climb it and set the trap in a suitable position. Then, just as you have safely regained the forest floor, your trap goes off with a triumphant clang, and the whole laborious process has to be endured once more. Thus, although trap-setting in the tree-tops is a painful necessity, you are always on the look-out for some slightly easier method of obtaining the animals you want. Probably one of the most successful and exciting of these methods is to smoke out the giant trees.

Some of the forest trees, although apparently sound and solid, are actually hollow for part or all of their length. These are the trees to look for, though they are not so easy to find. A day of searching in the forest might end with the discovery of six of them, perhaps one of which will yield good results when finally smoked out.

Smoking out a hollow tree is quite an art. To begin with, you must, if necessary, enlarge the opening at the base of the trunk and lay a small fire of dry twigs. Then two Africans are sent up the tree with nets to cover all the holes and cracks at the upper end of the trunk, and then station themselves at convenient points to catch any animals that emerge. When all is ready, you start the fire, and as soon as it is crackling you lay on top of the flames a large bundle of fresh green leaves. Immediately the flames die away and in their place rises a column of thick and pungent smoke. The great hollow interior of the tree acts like a gigantic chimney, and the smoke is whisked up inside. You never realize, until you light the fire, quite how many holes and cracks there are in the trunk of the tree. As you watch, you see a tiny tendril of smoke appear magically on the bark perhaps twenty feet from the ground, coiling out of an almost invisible hole; a short pause and ten feet higher three more little holes puff smoke like miniature cannon-mouths. Thus, guided by the tiny streamers of smoke appearing at intervals along the trunk, you can watch the progress of the smoking. If the tree is a good one, you have only time to watch the smoke get half-way up, for it is then that the animals start to break cover and you become very busy indeed.

When one of these hollow trees is inhabited, it is really like a block of flats. In the ground-floor apartments, for example, you find things like the giant land-snails, each the size of an apple, and they come gliding out of the base of the tree with all the speed a snail is capable of mustering, even in an emergency. They may be followed by other creatures who prefer the lower apartments or else are unable to climb: the big forest toads, for example, whose backs are cleverly marked out to resemble a dead leaf, and whose cheeks and sides are a beautiful mahogany red. They come waddling out from among the tree-tops with the most ludicrously indignant expressions on their faces, and on reaching the open air suddenly squat down and stare about them in a pathetic and helpless sort of way.

Having evicted all the ground-floor tenants, you then have to wait a short time before the occupants higher up have a chance to make their way down to the opening. Almost invariably giant millipedes are among the first to appear—charming creatures that look like brown sausages, with a fringe of legs along the underside of their bodies. They are quite harmless and rather imbecile creatures for which I have a very soft spot. One of their most ridiculous antics, when placed on a table, is to set off walking, all their legs working furiously, and on coming to the edge they never seem to notice it and continue to walk out into space until the weight of their body bends them over. Then, half on and half off the table, they pause, consider, and eventually decide that something is wrong. And so, starting with the extreme hind pair of legs, they go into reverse and get themselves on to the table again—only to crawl to the other side and repeat the performance.

Immediately after the appearance of the giant millipedes all the other top-floor tenants of the tree break cover together, some making for the top of the tree, others for the bottom. Perhaps there are squirrels with black ears, green bodies and tails of the most beautiful flame colour; giant grey dormice who gallop out of the tree, trailing their bushy tails behind them like puffs of smoke; perhaps a pair of bush-babies, with their great innocent eyes and their slender attenuated and trembly hands, like those of very old men. And then, of course, there are the bats: great fat brown bats with curious flower-like decorations on the skin of their noses and large transparent ears; others bright ginger, with black ears twisted down over their heads and pig-like snouts. And as this pageant of wild life appears the whip-scorpions are all over the place, skimming up and down the tree with a speed and silence that is unnerving and uncanny, squeezing their revolting bodies into the thinnest crack as you make a swipe at them with the net, only to reappear suddenly ten feet lower down the tree, skimming towards you apparently with the intention of disappearing into your shirt. You step back hurriedly and the creature vanishes: only the tips of a pair of antennae, wiggling from the depths of a crevice in the bark that would hardly accommodate a visiting-card, tells you of its whereabouts. Of the many creatures in the West African forest the whip-scorpion has been responsible for more shocks to my system than any other. The day a particularly large and leggy specimen ran over my bare arm, as I leant against a tree, will always be one of my most vivid memories. It took at least a year off my life.

But to return to Wilhelmina. She was a well-brought-up little whip-scorpion, one of a family of ten, and I started my intimate acquaintance with her when I captured her mother. All this happened quite by chance.

I had for many days been smoking out trees in the forest in search of an elusive and rare little animal known as the pigmy scaly-tail. These little mammals, which look like mice with long feathery tails, have a curious membrane of skin stretched from ankle to wrist, with the aid of which they glide around the forest with the ease of swallows. The scaly-tails live in colonies in hollow trees, but the difficulty lay in finding a tree that contained a colony. When, after much fruitless hunting, I did discover a group of these prizes, and moreover actually managed to capture some, I felt considerably elated. I even started to take a benign interest in the numerous whip-scorpions that were scuttling about the tree. Then suddenly I noticed one which looked so extraordinary, and was behaving in such a peculiar manner, that my attention was at once arrested. To begin with, this whip-scorpion seemed to be wearing a green fur-coat that almost completely covered her chocolate body. Secondly, it was working its way slowly and carefully down the tree with none of the sudden fits and starts common to the normal whip-scorpion.

Wondering if the green fur-coat and the slow walk were symptoms of extreme age in the whip-scorpion world I moved closer to examine the creature. To my astonishment I found that the fur-coat was composed of baby whip-scorpions, each not much larger than my thumb-nail, which were obviously fairly recent additions to the family. They were, in extraordinary contrast to their dark-coloured mother, a bright and bilious green, the sort of green that confectioners are fond of using in cake decorations. The mother's slow and stately progress was due to her concern lest one of her babies, lose its grip and drop off. I realized, rather ruefully, that I had never given the private life of the whip-scorpion much thought, and it had certainly never occurred to me that the female would be sufficiently maternal to carry her babies on her back. Overcome with remorse at my thoughtlessness, I decided that here was an ideal chance for me to catch up on my studies of these creatures. So I captured the female very carefully —to avoid dropping any of her progeny—and carried her back to camp.

I placed the mother and children in a large roomy box with plenty of cover in the way of bark and leaves. Every morning I had to look under these, rather gingerly I admit, to see if she was all right. At first, the moment I lifted the bark under which she was hiding, she would rush out and scuttle up the side of the box, a distressing habit which always made me jump and slam the lid down. I was very much afraid that one day I might do this and trap her legs or antennae, but fortunately after the first three days or so she settled down, and would even let me renew the leaves and bark in her box without taking any notice.

I had the female whip-scorpion and her babies for two months, and during that time the babies ceased to ride on their mother's back. They scattered and took up residence in various parts of the box, grew steadily and lost their green colouring in favour of brown. Whenever they grew too big for their skins they would split them down the back and step out of them, like spiders. Each time they did so they would emerge a little larger and a little browner. I discovered that while the mother would tackle anything from a small grass-hopper to a large beetle, the babies were fussy and demanded small spiders, slugs and other easily digestible fare. They all appeared to be thriving, and I began to feel rather proud of them. Then one day I returned to camp after a few hours hunting in the forest to find that tragedy had struck.

A tame Patas monkey I kept tied up outside the tent had eaten through his rope and been on a tour of investigation. Before anyone had noticed it he had eaten a bunch of bananas, three mangos and four hard-boiled eggs, he had broken two bottles of disinfectant, and rounded the whole thing off by knocking my whip-scorpion box on to the floor. It promptly broke open and scattered the family on the ground, and the Patas monkey, a creature of depraved habits, had set to work and eaten them. When I got back he was safely tied up again, and suffering from an acute attack of hiccups.

I picked up my whip-scorpion nursery and peered mournfully into it, cursing myself for having left it in such an accessible place, and cursing the monkey for having such an appetite. But then, to my surprise and delight, I found, squatting in solitary state on a piece of bark, one of the baby whip-scorpions, the sole survivor of the massacre. Tenderly I moved it to a smaller and more burglar-proof cage, showered it with slugs and other delicacies and christened it, for no reason at all, Wilhelmina.

During the time I had Wilhelmina's mother, and Wilhelmina herself, I learnt quite a lot about whip-scorpions. I discovered that though quite willing to hunt by day if hungry, they were at their most lively during the night. During the day Wilhelmina was always a little dull-witted, but in the evening she woke up and, if I may use the expression, blossomed. She would stalk to and fro in her box, her pincers at the ready, her long

The Patas monkey had set to work and eaten
them

antennae-like legs lashing out like whips ahead of her, seeking the best route. Although these tremendously elongated legs are supposed to be merely feelers, I got the impression that they could do more than this. I have seen them wave in the direction of an insect, pause and twitch, whereupon Wilhelmina would brace herself, almost as if she had smelt or heard her prey with the aid of her long legs. Sometimes she would stalk her food like this; at other times she would simply lie in wait until the unfortunate insect walked almost into her arms, and the powerful pincers would gather it lovingly into her mouth.

As she grew older I gave her bigger and bigger things to eat, and I found her courage extraordinary. She was rather like a pugnacious terrier who, the larger the opponent, the better he likes the fight. I was so fascinated by her skill and bravery in tackling insects as big or bigger than herself that one day, rather unwisely, I put a very large locust in with her. Without a moment's hesitation, she flew at him and grasped his bulky body in her pincers. To my alarm, however, the locust gave a hearty kick with his powerful hind legs and both he and Wilhelmina soared upwards and hit the wire-gauze roof of the cage with a resounding thump, then crashed back to the floor again. This rough treatment did not deter Wilhelmina at all, and she continued to hug the locust while he leapt wildly around the cage, thumping against the roof, until eventually he was exhausted. Then she settled down and made short work of him. But after this I was always careful to give her the smaller insects, for I had visions of a leg or one of her whips being broken off in such a rough contest.

By now I had become very fond and not a little proud of Wilhelmina. She was, as far as I knew, the only whip-scorpion to have been kept in captivity. What is more, she had become very tame. I had only to rap on the side of her box with my fingers and she would appear from under her piece of bark and wave her whips at me. Then, if I put my hand inside, she would climb on to my palm and sit there quietly while I fed her with slugs, creatures for which she still retained a passion.

When the time drew near for me to transport my large collection of animals back to England, I began to grow rather worried over Wilhelmina. It was a two-week voyage, and I could not take enough insect food for that length of time. I decided therefore to try making her eat raw meat. It took me a long time to achieve it, but once I had learnt the art of waggling the bit of meat seductively enough I found that Wilhelmina would grab it, and on this unlikely diet she seemed to thrive. On the journey down to the coast by lorry Wilhelmina behaved like a veteran traveller, sitting in her box and sucking a large chunk of raw meat almost throughout the trip. For the first day on board ship the strange surroundings made her a little sulky, but after that the sea air seemed to do her good and she became positively skittish. This was her undoing.

One evening when I went to feed her, she scuttled up as far as my elbow before I knew what was happening, dropped on to a hatch-cover and was just about to squeeze her way through a crack on a tour of investigation when I recovered from my astonishment and managed to grab her. For the next few days I fed her very cautiously, and she seemed to have quietened down and regained her former self-possession.

Then one evening she waggled her whips at me so plaintively that I lifted her out of her cage on the palm of my hand and started to feed her on the few remaining slugs I had brought for her in a tin. She ate two slugs, sitting quietly and decorously on my hand, and then suddenly she jumped. She could not have chosen a worse time, for as she was in mid-air a puff of wind swept round the bulkhead and whisked her away. I had a brief glimpse of her whips waving wildly, and then she was over the rail and gone, into the vast heaving landscape of the sea. I rushed to the rail and peered over, but it was impossible to spot so small a creature in the waves and froth below. Hurriedly I threw her box over, in the vain hope that she might find it and use it as a raft. A ridiculous hope, I know, but I did not like to think of her drowning without making some attempt to save her. I could have kicked myself for my stupidity in lifting her out of her box; I never thought I would have been so affected by the loss of such a creature. I had grown very fond of her; she in her turn had seemed to trust me. It was a tragic way for the relationship to end. But there was one slight consolation: after my association with Wilhelmina I shall never again look at a whip-scorpion with quite the same distaste.

The Ants

H. H. Ewers

Every one who has lived in the tropics can tell stories
about Ant armies which have paid him a visit at night.
The Gypsy Ants may fear only the largest human cities,
yet they seem to feel the obligation, from time to time,
to see what they can get out of human nests. The bedposts are set in saucers containing vinegar or petroleum.
If, on account of the heat of the night the sleeper has not
thrown off the coverings, so that they hang down to the
floor, he is safe from the invading hosts while in bed. I
have enjoyed more than one of these visits, and managed
to make my escape. We gradually learn how to act
properly as host. But my first night with these dark
maidens was bad enough. I shall not forget it, no
matter how long I may live.

We had been drinking pulque, which is maguey
whisky, preferred by the Mexicans above all other
drinks. It has a horrible flavour and the head you get
next morning is awful—but you must try anything
once if you are travelling all over the world as a writer.
I have drunk worse in my time. First you are very lively
and then most emotional. We had been sitting for a
long time, and had drunk considerable pulque.

Then I went home. I lived in a one-storey bungalow

which the owner styled a 'chalet'. I was taken care of by an old Indian woman. I did not go to bed at once, but sat down by the writing-table. I felt the uncontrollable urge to pen a sonnet—a sonnet to a Singsong girl I had met in Hankow, who certainly would not understand a word of it. If she had heard of the sonnet, she would certainly have attributed it to alcohol; but she was devoted to Saki, not to pulque—to rice-whisky, not maguey-whisky. I dreamt of her, and I wrote four lines about the sins of her slender fingers—and then four lines more; then three lines. . . . The last three lines I never wrote. The ladies came a-visiting—and I forgot her little finger, the Singsong girl, pulque and sonnet.

I heard a dim peep, peep. Then the peeping became louder; the peeping was intense. I jumped up, looked around; saw the floor covered with a black carpet. But this carpet was alive. It moved and crawled—many thousand black Ants. Half the floor of the room was covered with them, and still more were coming in. Like waves the black masses rolled in. Instinctively I jumped up on my chair. The peeping never stopped. Very fine, thin, many voiced; then a stronger, sharper, fearful peeping.

I listened. It came from behind the cupboard. Yes, behind the cupboard was a Mouse-hole and a Mouse-nest in which lived Mamma Mouse and her Mouse children. I had heard them often as they squeaked, the little ones seeming to say: 'Bring us something good to eat!' And the Mouse-mamma seeming to ask me: 'Haven't you anything for me?' Every day I had shared my breakfast with her, giving her bread, cheese-rinds and sausage-casings. I called her Ignatz. She was a nice, lovely Mouse-mamma. Now she was being eaten up alive, she and her naked Mouse-children. There is no escape when the black six-leggers come.

They climbed my chair—ten, twenty, a hundred. Did they want to make me their prey? What did these blind things know of how large I was? Mouse or Man, all the same to them. I stepped on the table. My head whirled, but not from the pulque. A repulsive stench arose from the blackies, as of carrion, seeming to penetrate the pores of the skin, eating through clothing and skin. They came up on the table after me. They climbed all four legs of the table, swarming all over the chair as well. Its back was several inches from the table. At least those creatures could not reach me. I pulled out my handkerchief, wanting to sweep away all that reached the top of the table. They were coming over the edge, first a few, then more and more. I swept them off, balancing myself carefully. Wherever they appeared I hurled them down into that black, moving sea.

If only those Mice were dead at last, thought I, but they squeaked, and squeaked, ever more wildly, uncannily, hopelessly. Then I looked at the chair. It was entirely covered, legs, seat and back, but above where the curved back stood a little higher than the table, I saw a rare drama. Garlands of Ants were hanging there, as thick as your thumb—garlands of Ants! And I saw how their ranks grew, how one worker hung to the other. It was fascinating. I stood motionless staring down at the creatures. I knew that they were blind, that they could not see at all, yet they were coming from the chair to the table, forming a living ladder—

Now the first Ants reached the table and poured over a matchbox. Then the black hosts swarmed upon the ladder, and poured themselves all over the table. At the same time those climbing up the four legs of the table appeared, and the black flood rolled over the edge from every side. A second chain was completed from the chair to the table. I had to make but a single motion to hurl them to the floor, but the idea never occurred to me.

But I had to get away—the smell of carrion was more horrible than ever. In the next few moments they must reach me—I was nauseated at the thought. Hardly two feet from the table was the washstand and in the centre of it stood the large pewter pitcher filled with water. There I would be safe. . . . One step. . . . I stood on the washstand, and in another I had both feet in the enormous pitcher. I noticed that the washstand was already covered with ants. Did they want to find out what soap tasted like? I had stepped among the blackies with my left foot, taking a half dozen into the pitcher with me. I fished them out of the water carefully.

It was a frightful pewter pitcher in which I stood. I had worried over it for a fortnight. Now I was very glad indeed that it was not china, which would certainly have broken. I stood straight as a candle, foot to foot. I will not say that it was very comfortable. I had to stand very carefully so as to preserve my equilibrium. Sometimes I lifted the right foot, then the left, in order to rest a little.

The army continued to stream into the room under the door. They covered everything now, creeping into my trunk, climbing on the sofa, clinging to the walls, here and there. They were more and more by the minute. It seemed to me that they were in layers, as if the black waves down there were rising higher. It is certain that they were climbing the sides of the pewter pitcher, and already were running around the edge. I could hardly bear my cramped position any longer. What if I were to jump down and leap for the door? Run down the steps and out of the house?

But I had the feeling that I would sink up to the knees in those black waves. I knew that it was unreasonable; knew very well that the Ants covered the floor only a fraction of an inch. Nevertheless I felt as if I would go in up to my knees. A stumble; slipping in the crushed mass; falling in the midst of them; the black, living sea swarming over me! Now, for the first time I became worried. I would not look at the Ants any more; I closed both eyes. But that peep, peep of the Mice which they were eating alive—and this gruesome odour of carrion and garbage. It seemed to me almost as if they had taken fast hold of me, as if my body, my own breath were emitting this disgusting odour. My head swam. I reeled, opened my eyes again, stood straight with the very last atom of will power.

Then I saw how the blackies were coming into the water. They hung on the edge of the pitcher, one after the other and dropped into the water, as they built a bridge over to me, just as they had constructed a ladder from the back of the chair to the top of the table. For a minute I was very still, watching them as they worked, seeing how they lengthened their living bridge, coming nearer and nearer to my leg. I could almost calculate how long it would take them to get there. . . . And again I became dizzy. The fearful squeaking of the Mice rang in my ears; the disgusting stench was sticky in my nostrils. My eyes smarted at sight of the black swaying waves. I thought that I felt the Ants crawling all over my body and biting me in a thousand places. It seemed to me that my mouth was filled with the black things. My tongue was parched, twisting with the awful struggle. Fear, fear—and a cold sweat! One loud shout of despair—then I jumped!

I do not know why I did not do that sooner, nor do I know why I did it just at that moment. My bed was very close, hardly a yard from the washstand. I might have saved myself long before. I made one leap into the middle of the bed. Without thinking I crept under the sheet and wrapped myself in it. I gasped—breathed—all danger was past. I knew that I was safe there. The four bedposts stood in pewter saucers filled with kerosene—not a black beast dared come near.

I closed my eyes again, held my nostrils. Still that squeaking, but weaker, slowly weakening. Other rustlings, which I could not explain to myself, from other creatures done to death, like the Mice. Then came the sharp cry of a Bird. At once it came to me that this was the Blackbird in its cage, belonging to the Indian woman. Would they eat him too? I wrapped my head in the covers—only to hear, see, smell nothing more.

* * *

The next morning the old woman brought me my breakfast to the bedside. She had great difficulty in awakening me; she did so most unwillingly, only because I had given the strictest orders. At once I thought of the night and the Ants. I looked around but saw nothing strange. Had I dreamed all that? I asked the old woman if she had noticed nothing during the night. She nodded, smiling. Certainly, the 'Tepeguas' had been there. She knew it at once. Whenever her bird screamed at night, Tepeguas had put in an appearance. She appeared highly pleased over their visit: no more vermin in the house, not a Rat or a Mouse, not a Lizard, a Spider, a Centipede, Lice, or Cockroaches. The bungalow had been eaten clean. The Tepeguas were excellent house-cleaners.

'But your Bird, your Blackbird?' She laughed. 'Him? What could they do to him? His cage hung from the ceiling by a thin wire. No, he ate the Tepeguas—that was the reason he was so glad and screamed when they came in.' She had gathered a couple of handfuls of them, and brought them in; a few that had remained behind lying near a Snake, of which nothing but the skeleton remained. Poor Snake, thought I, such a beautiful animal, with his blue markings and golden eyes. I had caught him a few days before in the forest, and put him into a wooden box, under the steps leading into the bungalow.

But now I must get up. My guide was below, waiting with the horses. When I came back in the evening all would have been washed up; strong-scented flowers would be there, so that I would not notice that strong odour of the Tepeguas.

THE ANT

Ogden Nash

The ant has made himself illustrious
Through constant industry industrious.
So what?
Would you be calm and placid
If you were full of formic acid?

THE TERMITE

Ogden Nash

Some primal termite knocked on wood
And tasted it, and found it good,
And that is why your Cousin May
Fell through the parlour floor today.

Horrors of
the Deep

The Legends of the Kraken and The Hydra

Lucy Berman

Are there such things as sea-serpents? Is there a Loch Ness Monster? People have argued for centuries about the existence of strange creatures in lakes and seas. Sea-monster legends have grown up in every seafaring nation. Some creatures once believed to be legendary have been proved to have a basis in fact. One of these creatures was the *kraken* and another was the *hydra*.

The kraken was a huge monster, first described by Norwegian writers. In 1555, Olaus Magnus wrote: 'Their Forms are horrible, their Heads square, all set with prickles, and they have sharp and long horns round about, like a Tree rooted up by the Roots . . . one of these Sea-Monsters will drown easily many great ships provided with many strong Mariners.'

Two hundred years later the legend had become greatly exaggerated. A fair-sized kraken was said to be one-and-a-half miles in circumference! Stories were told of sailors who landed on a kraken, believing it to be an island. They settled themselves for the night and built a fire, whereupon the monster sank below the surface, leaving them to swim for their lives.

Erik Pontoppidan, an eighteenth century Norwegian bishop, described the kraken surfacing: 'At last several bright points or horns appear, which grow thicker and thicker the higher they rise above the surface of the water, and sometimes they stand up as high as the masts of middle-sized vessels. It seems these are the creature's arms, and, it is said, if they were to lay hold of the largest man-of-war, they would pull it to the bottom.'

One account of the kraken legend was that there were only two of these creatures. They were said to be as old as the world and to be doomed to die and to rise to the surface on the day that the world ended. The more usual accounts, however, claimed an innumerable population of krakens in the sea, which was an ever-present danger to sailors.

At the beginning of the nineteenth century, a French naturalist named Denis de Montfort described how a kraken (which he called a *poulpe colossal* or 'colossal octopus') wrapped its arms around a three-masted ship and nearly succeeded in pulling it to the bottom of the sea. He had no evidence for this story other than a picture on a church wall, but he used his imagination and invented a struggle in which the crew only just saved themselves by cutting off the monster's arms. His story was a sensation, and its success prompted him to even wilder imaginings. He published an account of the sinkings of ten ships in a single night by a whole school of *poulpes colossal*.

No one believed this second account. Both de Montfort and the kraken were discredited. In 1861, however, a real ship named the *Alecton* had a real encounter with a kraken. The animal tried to keep at a fair distance from the ship, but the captain decided to harpoon it. He managed to tie it to the side, but it broke away, leaving a portion of its tail behind. It was described as having a body fifteen to eighteen feet long, and a head with a parrot-like beak surrounded by powerful arms five to six feet in length. The arms were equipped with strong suckers, and the captain felt that a close encounter with these arms could be very dangerous. His men wanted to pursue the creature in a small boat, but he refused.

When the *Alecton* story was published, few people could doubt it. The evidence was very detailed and supported by many witnesses. The captain of the *Alecton* declared that he had seen Denis de Montfort's *poulpe colossal*. He said that it was not a myth, but was in fact a giant-sized squid. Seafaring people were quite familiar with small squids. They recognized easily the slender body, the head with its sharp beak surrounded by eight arms and two longer tentacles. But previous to the *Alecton* incident, accounts of giant squid-like creatures had been relegated to the realms of myth and fancy.

It was not until the early 1870's that the existence of the giant squid was accepted as fact by scientists. From about 1870 to 1879, giant squids by the dozens were stranded off Nova Scotia. Scientists were able to measure and classify actual specimens. The largest one found measured fifty-seven feet overall, including tentacles forty-nine feet three inches in length. The scientists also studied accounts of the kraken and the *poulpe colossal*, and they concluded that the legendary and the real creatures were one and the same animal.

* * *

The case of the hydra is far less detailed than that of the kraken. The hydra was a monster in Greek mythology. It lived in a swamp near the well of Amyone, from which it frightened people away. The hero Hercules was sent to destroy it, but his task was difficult, for the hydra had nine heads, of which the middle one was immortal. Hercules attacked the monster with a club. He knocked off several of its heads, but as soon as one fell, two more grew in its place! At last, with the help of his servant, he burned away all but the immortal head, and that one he buried under a vast pile of rock.

The animal on which the legend of the hydra was based was almost certainly the octopus. An octopus has eight arms springing from a large head. These arms are the equivalent of the hydra's eight 'ordinary' heads, while the octopus' head is represented in the legend by the ninth or immortal head. It is a fact that when an octopus loses an arm, it grows a new one. Octopuses are often found with one or more small, thin arms in process of regrowth. This ability of the octopus to re-generate parts of itself could easily have given rise to the legend of a creature that grew two heads for every one that was chopped off.

Statues of Hercules and the hydra dating from Roman days show the hydra as looking very much like an octopus. Several hundred years later, however, this identification had been forgotten. Renaissance natura-lists disagreed over whether the hydra was a real or an imaginary animal. The octopus itself, although a familiar creature in many parts of the world, was greatly ignored by scientists. Aristotle had described the octopus and its relatives three hundred years before Christ, but during the next 2,000 years there were no detailed scientific studies of octopuses.

In 1866, Victor Hugo published his novel, *Toilers of The Sea*, in which he described a battle between his hero, Gilliatt, and an octopus, in a cave in the Channel Islands. Suddenly the octopus was a sensation. Newspapers pub-lished stories of how dangerous octopuses were. The aquarium in Paris acquired an octopus which people flocked to see. Restaurants featured octopus meat on the menu. All this attention was followed by more serious study, and it was not long before the octopus was once again identified as the source of the legend of the hydra.

The Squids

Jules Verne

For some days the submarine gave the American coast a wide berth. Captain Nemo evidently did not wish to encounter the waves of the Gulf of Mexico or of the Antilles Seas. There was no want of water there, for the average depth is about 1,800 yards; but probably the islands, with which the seas are studded, did not recommend them to the captain.

On the 16th April we sighted Martinique and Guadeloupe at thirty miles distance. I saw the high peaks for a moment.

The Canadian, who had counted upon putting his plans of escape into execution in the Gulf—either by landing on some island, or by hailing one of the numerous vessels which ply from one island to another—was very much put out.

Flight would have been practicable had Ned been able to get possession of the boat without the captain's knowledge; but, in the open sea, it was useless to think of it.

Ned, Conseil, and I had a long conversation on this subject. We had now been six months on board the *Nautilus*, we had sailed 17,000 leagues, and, as Ned remarked, it was time to put an end to it. He suggested that we should go and put the question boldly to Captain Nemo whether he intended to keep us on board for ever?

But to this I would not agree. We had nothing to hope from the captain, we must trust to ourselves. Besides, for some time he had become gloomy, reserved, and unsociable. He seemed to avoid me; I only encountered him at rare intervals. Formerly he seemed pleased to be able to explain the wonders of the sea; now he left me to my studies in the saloon.

What change was come upon him, and why? I had no reason to reproach myself. Perhaps our presence on board worried him. Nevertheless, I did not think he would give us our liberty,

I therefore begged Ned to pause before acting. If this attempt had no result it would only revive his suspicions, and render our position unpleasant, and injurious to the projects of the Canadian. I will add that I could adduce no argument on the score of health. If I except the rough experience beneath the iceberg, we had never been better in our lives. The healthy food, the pure air, and regularity of our lives, with the uniformity of temperature, gave illness no chance, and for a man who did not regret the world, or—like Captain Nemo, who was at home, who went where he chose—I could understand the pleasure of such an existence. But for us, we had not broken with mankind. I did not wish to bury with me my curious and novel studies. I had now the right to write a true book of the sea, and I wished sooner or later to have it published.

On the 20th April we had risen to a medium height of 1,500 yards. The nearest land was the Bahamas, lying like a number of paving-stones at the surface of the sea. High cliffs rose up, perpendicular walls, rough blocks placed in long layers, amongst which were deep holes to the end of which our electric light could not penetrate. These rocks were clothed with immense sea-grasses and weeds, hydrophytes worthy of a Titan world.

From speaking of enormous plants Ned and Conseil naturally turned to gigantic animals in the sea. The former were evidently intended to nourish the latter; while from the windows of the saloon I did not see any but the principal articulates of the division of brachiousa, long-footed lampreys, violet crabs, and clios, peculiar to the Antilles.

About 11 a.m. Ned Land directed my attention to the extraordinary amount of movement going on amongst the algae.

'Well,' I said, 'they are the regular caves of squids or cuttle-fish, and I should not be surprised to see one of those monsters.'

'What!' cried Conseil, 'ordinary cuttle-fish of the class of cephalopods?'

'No,' I replied, 'but cuttle-fish of enormous size. But perhaps friend Ned is mistaken, for I can perceive none of them.'

'I am sorry for it. I should like to see one of those monsters of which I have heard, which are able to drag ships under water. They are called krak—'

'It *is* a regular "cracker", altogether, I should think,' said Ned; ' "cracker" will do!'

'Krakens!' replied Conseil, having got out the word without noticing his companion's 'chaff.'

'You will never make me believe that such animals exist,' said Ned.

'Why not?' exclaimed Conseil, 'you believed Monsieur's narwhal.'

'We were wrong, Conseil.'

'No doubt, but other people believe it still.'

'It is probable, Conseil; but I have made up my mind not to admit the existence of these monsters till I have dissected them myself,' said I.

'So,' replied Conseil, 'Monsieur does not believe in these gigantic "octopi"?'

'Why, who the devil *has* ever believed in them?' asked Ned.

'Lots of people, friend Ned.'

'No fishermen; *savants* perhaps may!'

'Excuse me, Ned, both fishermen and *savants*.'

'But,' said Conseil, with the most serious air in the world, 'I perfectly remember to have seen a large ship pulled down beneath the waves by one of the arms of a cuttle.'

'You have seen that!' exclaimed the Canadian.

'Yes, Ned.'

'With your own eyes?'

'With my own eyes.'

'And where, if you please?'

'At St. Malo,' replied the imperturbable Conseil.

'In the harbour, I suppose,' said Ned, ironically.

'No, in a church.'

'In a church!' exclaimed Ned.

'Yes, there is a picture there, representing the cuttle.'

'Capital!' cried Ned, laughing. 'Conseil did puzzle me a bit.'

'As a fact, he is quite right,' I said. 'I have heard of that picture, but the subject is taken from a legend, and you know what to think of legends, when applied to natural history. Besides, when monsters are in question, the imagination is apt to run wild a little. Not only has it been stated that these cuttles can drag ships down, but a certain Olaüs Magnus speaks of a cephalopod a mile long, which was more like an island than an animal. It is also recounted that the Bishop of Nidros one day built an altar upon an enormous rock. Mass concluded, the rock got up and departed to the sea. The rock was a cuttle!'

'Is that all?' said Ned.

'No; another bishop, Pontoppidan de Berghem, also speaks of a cuttle upon which he could exercise a regiment of cavalry!'

'They said something besides their prayers, did those bishops,' replied Ned.

'Finally, the ancient naturalists quote monsters whose throats were like gulfs, and which were too large to get through the Straits of Gibraltar.'

'Oh! go ahead!' said the Canadian.

'But now, what is the truth of all this?' asked Conseil.

'Nothing, my friends—nothing at least which passes the limits of truth and reaches legend or fable. Still, there is at any rate some ground or pretext for this play of the imagination of story-tellers. One cannot deny that cuttles and squids of great size do exist, but they are not so large as whales. Aristotle mentioned a squid of five cubits, nearly ten yards in length. Fishermen have often met with them more than four feet long. The museums of Trieste and Montpellier have skeletons of such creatures measuring two yards. Besides, according to the calculation of naturalists, one of these animals, measuring six feet only, has tentacles twenty-seven feet in length. That would be a formidable monster!'

'Do they fish for them at present?' asked Ned Land.

'If they do not fish for them, sailors see them. One of my friends, Captain Paul Bos, of Havre, has often told me that he met an enormous cuttle in the Indian seas. But the most astonishing incident, and one that will not allow us to deny the existence of these animals, happened in 1861.'

'How was that?' asked Ned.

'In 1861, at the north-east of Teneriffe, not far from where we are now, the crew of the despatch-vessel, *Alecto*, perceived an enormous cuttle. Captain Bonguer approached it, and attacked it with harpoons and guns, without any marked success, for both bullets and harpoons recoiled from its flesh, which is like soft jelly. After many attempts they succeeded in fastening a rope round the animal's body. The noose slipped to the caudal fins, and there it stopped. They then attempted to haul the monster on board, but his weight was so enormous that the tail was separated from the body, and, deprived of this ornament, the cuttle disappeared beneath the waves.'

'At length we have a fact,' said Ned Land.

'An indisputable fact. So it was proposed to name the creature the "Bonguer cuttle-fish." '

'How long was it?' asked the Canadian.

'Did it not measure about six yards?' said Conseil, who was posted at the window, watching the fissures in the cliffs.

'Precisely,' I replied.

'Was not its head crowned with eight tentacles, which moved about in the water like a nest of serpents?'

'Quite so,' I replied.

'Were not the eyes placed at the back of the head and very large?'

'Yes, Conseil.'

'And was its mouth like a parrot's beak, but a very terrible one?'

'Quite true, Conseil.'

'Well, then, if Monsieur pleases,' replied Conseil, quietly, 'if yonder is not Bonguer's cuttle-fish, it is one of the family.'

I gazed at Conseil. Ned Land rushed to the window.

'The horrible beast!' he cried.

I in my turn came to look, and could not repress a shudder of disgust. Before my eyes was a fearful monster, worthy to figure in legends of the marvellous.

It was a squid of enormous dimensions, eight yards

Before my eyes was a fearful monster . . .

long. It moved sideways with extreme velocity in the direction of the *Nautilus*. It gazed at us with its enormous staring sea-green eyes. Its eight arms, or rather its eight feet, were fixed to its head, which gives these animals the name of cephalopods—were double the length of its body, and turned about like the head-dress of the furies. We could distinctly see the 250 air-holes on the inner side of the 'arms,' shaped like semi-spherical capsules. Sometimes these air-holes fastened against the window, and thus emptied themselves. The monster's mouth, a horny beak like that of a parrot, opened vertically. Its horny tongue, itself armed with many ranges of sharp teeth, came quivering from out those veritable shears. What a freak of Nature this—a bird's beak on a mollusc! Its body shaped like a spindle, and swollen in the middle, formed a fleshy mass which must have weighed 40,000 or 50,000 lbs. Its colour changed with great rapidity, according to the irritation of the animal, passing successively from a livid grey to a reddish-brown tinge.

What irritated the mollusc? No doubt the presence of the *Nautilus*, more formidable than itself, and on which its beak and tentacles had no effect. What monsters these squids are, what vitality they possess, what vigour they must have in their movements, since they have three hearts!

Chance had brought us in contact with this creature, and I did not wish to lose the opportunity to study the specimen carefully. I overcame the horror with which its appearance inspired me, and, seizing a pencil, I commenced to make a sketch of it.

'Perhaps this is the same that the *Alecto* encountered,' said Conseil.

'No,' said the Canadian, 'because this one is complete; the other fellow had lost a tail.'

'This is no reason,' I replied; 'these animals can reform their arms and tail by redintegration, and in seven years the tail of Bonguer's cuttle, no doubt, has had time to grow again.'

'Besides,' replied Ned, 'if this be not the one, it may be one of those others.'

As he spoke other squids appeared at the window. I counted seven of them. They attended on the *Nautilus*, and I heard the grinding of their beaks on the iron hull. We had enough now at any rate.

I continued my work. The monsters kept their places with such precision that they appeared immovable, and I was able to draw them foreshortened on the glass; besides, we were not going fast.

Suddenly the *Nautilus* stopped. A shock was felt all through her frame.

'What have we struck?' I exclaimed.

'In any case we are free, for we are floating,' said the Canadian.

The *Nautilus* was floating, certainly, but it was not moving. The screw was not going. A minute passed, when Captain Nemo and his mate entered.

I had not seen the captain for some time; he seemed preoccupied. Without speaking, perhaps without seeing us, he went to the panel, looked at the squids, and said something to the mate.

The latter went out; the panels were soon closed, and the ceiling was lighted. I approached the captain.

'A curious collection,' I said, in the easy way a person might speak of them in an aquarium.

'Yes, indeed, professor, and we are going to fight them hand to hand.'

I looked at the captain, not thinking I had heard aright.

'Hand to hand?' I repeated.

'Yes, the screw is stopped; I think one of their horny beaks has seized it. That is why we cannot move.'

'And what are you going to do?'

'Rise to the surface and kill the vermin.'

'Rather difficult, won't it?'

'Yes, indeed, for the electric bullets do not meet with sufficient resistance in their pulpy bodies to take effect.'

'But we shall attack them with hatchets.'

'And a harpoon,' suggested the Canadian, 'if you will accept my assistance.'

'I do, Master Land.'

'We will accompany you,' I said; and, with Captain Nemo, we advanced to the staircase.

There a dozen men, armed with boarding hatchets, were in readiness for the attack. Conseil and I armed ourselves likewise. Ned Land seized a harpoon.

The *Nautilus* now floated at the surface. One of the sailors, placed on the top of the ladder, unscrewed the bolts of the panel. But the screws were scarcely loosened when the panel was wrenched violently open, evidently drawn in by the suckers of a squid.

Immediately one of the long arms glided through the aperture, and twenty others were moving above. With a single blow Captain Nemo cut off this formidable tentacle, which slid writhing down the ladder.

As we were pressing forward together to reach the platform, two other arms, circling in the air, fell upon a sailor who was in front of Captain Nemo, and raised him up with irresistible power.

Captain Nemo uttered a shout, and rushed in front; we followed.

What a sight it was! The unhappy sailor, seized by the tentacle and fixed upon the sucker, was balanced in the air by this enormous 'trunk.' He gasped; he was almost stifled; and cried out 'Help, help!' These words, *pronounced in French*, astonished me greatly. I had a fellow-countryman on board—several perhaps. I shall hear that heart-rending appeal all my life.

The poor fellow was lost! Who could tear him from such a grasp as that? Nevertheless Captain Nemo threw himself upon the squid, and cut off one arm at a blow. The mate waged a terrible fight with others, which were assailing the sides of the *Nautilus*. The ship's company fought with hatchets. The Canadian, Conseil, and I wearied our arms hacking at these fleshy masses. A strong odour of musk pervaded the air. The scene was horrible.

For a moment I hoped that the unfortunate sailor seized by the squid would be released. Seven of the eight arms had been cut off. Only one, now brandishing like a feather twined aloft. But as Captain Nemo and his mate both rushed at the big animal it ejected a column of black liquid, secreted in a bag near the abdomen, at them. They were blinded, and when they recovered the squid had disappeared with our unfortunate friend.

Enraged against the monsters, we rushed pell-mell amongst ten or a dozen which had now gained the platform and sides of the *Nautilus*, which were soon covered with waves of inky blood. The viscous tentacles seemed to spring up like hydra heads. Ned Land, at each thrust of his harpoon, blinded the great staring eyes. But my companion was suddenly overturned by the tentacles of a monster that he had not been able to avoid. My heart beat wildly. The beak of the squid was extended over Ned Land. He would be cut in half. I rushed to his assistance. But Captain Nemo anticipated me. He flung his hatchet between the enormous mandibles, and the Canadian, miraculously rescued, plunged his harpoon into the triple heart of the squid.

'I owe myself that revenge,' said the captain to Ned Land.

Ned bowed, but made no reply.

The fight had lasted a quarter of an hour. The monsters, conquered, mutilated, beaten to death, left us at last, and disappeared.

Captain Nemo, red with blood, stood motionless near the lantern, gazed into the sea which had swallowed up one of his companions, and great tears stood in his eyes.

The Octopus

Victor Hugo

When he awakened he was hungry.

The sea was growing calmer. But there was still a heavy swell, which made his departure, for the present at least, impossible. The day, too, was far advanced. For the sloop with its burden to get to Guernsey before midnight, it was necessary to start in the morning.

Although pressed by hunger, Gilliatt began by stripping himself, the only means of getting warmth. His clothing was saturated by the storm, but the rain had washed out the sea-water, which rendered it possible to dry them.

He kept nothing on but his trousers, which he turned up nearly to the knees.

His overcoat, jacket, overalls, and sheepskin he spread out and fixed with large round stones here and there.

Then he thought of eating.

He had recourse to his knife, which he was careful to sharpen, and to keep always in good condition; and he detached from the rocks a few limpets, similar in kind to the *clonisses* of the Mediterranean. It is well known that these are eaten raw: but after so many labours, so various and so rude, the pittance was meagre. His biscuit was gone; but of water he had now abundance.

He took advantage of the receding tide to wander among the rocks in search of crayfish. There was extent enough of rock to hope for a successful search.

But he had not reflected that he could do nothing with these without fire to cook them. If he had taken the trouble to go to his store-cavern, he would have found it inundated with the rain. His wood and coal were drowned, and of his store of tow, which served him for tinder, there was not a fibre which was not saturated. No means remained of lighting a fire.

For the rest, his blower was completely disorganised. The screen of the hearth of his forge was broken down; the storm had sacked and devastated his workshop. With what tools and apparatus had escaped the general wreck, he could still have done carpentry work; but he could not have accomplished any of the labours of the smith. Gilliatt, however, never thought of his workshop for a moment.

Drawn in another direction by the pangs of hunger, he had pursued without much reflection his search for food. He wandered, not in the gorge of the rocks, but outside among the smaller breakers. It was there that the *Durande*, ten weeks previously, had first struck upon the sunken reef.

For the search that Gilliatt was prosecuting, this part was more favourable than the interior. At low water the crabs are accustomed to crawl out into the air. They seem to like to warm themselves in the sun, where they swarm sometimes to the disgust of loiterers, who recognise in these creatures, with their awkward sidelong gait, climbing clumsily from crack to crack the lower stages of the rocks like the steps of a staircase, a sort of sea vermin.

For two months Gilliatt had lived upon these vermin of the sea.

On this day, however, the crayfish and crabs were both wanting. The tempest had driven them into their solitary retreats; and they had not yet mustered courage to venture abroad. Gilliatt held his open knife in his hand, and from time to time scraped a cockle from under the bunches of seaweed, which he ate while still walking.

He could not have been far from the very spot where Sieur Clubin had perished.

As Gilliatt was determining to content himself with the sea-urchins and the *châtaignes de mer*, a little clattering noise at his feet aroused his attention. A large crab, startled by his approach, had just dropped into a pool. The water was shallow, and he did not lose sight of it.

He chased the crab along the base of the rock; the crab moved fast.

Suddenly it was gone.

It had buried itself in some crevice under the rock.

Gilliatt clutched the projections of the rock, and stretched out to observe where it shelved away under the water.

As he suspected, there was an opening there in which the creature had evidently taken refuge. It was more than a crevice; it was a kind of porch.

The sea entered beneath it, but was not deep. The bottom was visible, covered with large pebbles. The pebbles were green and clothed with *confervae*, indicating that they were never dry. They were like the tops of a number of heads of infants, covered with a kind of green hair.

Holding his knife between his teeth, Gilliatt descended, by the help of feet and hands, from the upper part of the escarpment, and leaped into the water. It reached almost to his shoulders.

He made his way through the porch, and found himself in a blind passage, with a roof in the form of a rude arch over his head. The walls were polished and slippery. The crab was nowhere visible. He gained his feet and advanced in daylight growing fainter, so that he began to lose the power to distinguish objects.

At about fifteen paces the vaulted roof ended overhead. He had penetrated beyond the blind passage. There was here more space, and consequently more daylight. The pupils of his eyes, moreover, had dilated; he could see pretty clearly. He was taken by surprise.

He had made his way again into the singular cavern which he had visited in the previous month. The only difference was that he had entered by the way of the sea.

It was through the submarine arch, that he had remarked before, that he had just entered. At certain low tides it was accessible.

His eyes became more accustomed to the place. His vision became clearer and clearer. He was astonished. He found himself again in that extraordinary palace of shadows; saw again before his eyes that vaulted roof, those columns, those purple and blood-like stains, that vegetation rich with gems, and at the farther end, that crypt or sanctuary, and that altar-like stone. He took little notice of these details, but their impression was in his mind, and he saw that the place was unchanged.

He observed before him, at a certain height in the wall, the crevice through which he had penetrated the first time, and which, from the point where he now stood, appeared inaccessible.

Near the moulded arch, he remarked those low dark grottoes, a sort of caves within a cavern, which he had already observed from a distance. He now stood nearer to them. The entrance to the nearest to him was out of the water, and easily approachable. Nearer still than this recess he noticed, above the level of the water, and within reach of his hand, a horizontal fissure. It seemed to him probable that the crab had taken refuge there, and he plunged his hand in as far as he was able, and groped about in that dusky aperture.

Suddenly he felt himself seized by the arm. A strange indescribable horror thrilled through him.

Some living thing, thin, rough, flat, cold, slimy, had twisted itself round his naked arm, in the dark depth below. It crept upward towards his chest. Its pressure was like a tightening cord, its steady persistence like that of a screw. In less than a moment some mysterious spiral form had passed round his wrist and elbow, and had reached his shoulder. A sharp point penetrated beneath the armpit.

Gilliatt recoiled; but he had scarcely power to move! He was, as it were, nailed to the place. With his left hand, which was disengaged, he seized his knife, which he still held between his teeth, and with that hand, holding the knife, he supported himself against the rocks, while he made a desperate effort to withdraw his arm. He succeeded only in disturbing his persecutor, which wound itself still tighter. It was supple as leather, strong as steel, cold as night.

A second form, sharp, elongated, and narrow, issued out of the crevice, like a tongue of monstrous jaws. It seemed to lick his naked body. Then suddenly stretching out, it became longer and thinner, as it crept over his skin, and wound itself round him. At the same time a terrible sense of pain, comparable to nothing he had ever known, compelled all his muscles to contract. He felt upon his skin a number of flat rounded points. It seemed as if innumerable suckers had fastened to his flesh and were about to drink his blood.

A third long undulating shape issued from the hole in

the rock; seemed to feel its way about his body; lashed round his ribs like a cord, and fixed itself there.

Agony when at its height is mute. Gilliatt uttered no cry. There was sufficient light for him to see the repulsive forms which had entangled themselves about him. A fourth ligature, but this one swift as an arrow, darted towards his stomach, and wound around him there.

It was impossible to sever or tear away the slimy bands were twisted tightly round his body, and were adhering by a number of points. Each of the points was the focus of frightful and singular pangs. It was as if numberless small mouths were devouring him at the same time.

A fifth long, slimy, riband-shaped strip issued from the hole. It passed over the others, and wound itself tightly around his chest. The compression increased his sufferings. He could scarcely breathe.

These living thongs were pointed at their extremities, but broadened like a blade of a sword towards its hilt. All belonged evidently to the same centre. They crept and glided about him; he felt the strange points of pressure, which seemed to him like mouths, change their places from time to time.

Suddenly a large, round, flattened, glutinous mass issued from beneath the crevice. It was the centre; the five thongs were attached to it like spokes to the nave of a wheel. On the opposite side of this disgusting monster appeared the commencement of three other tentacles, the ends of which remained under the rock. In the middle of this slimy mass appeared two eyes.

The eyes were fixed on Gilliatt.

He recognised the Devil-Fish.

It is difficult for those who have not seen it to believe in the existence of the devil-fish.

Compared to this creature, the ancient hydras are insignificant.

At times we are tempted to imagine that the vague forms which float in our dreams may encounter in the realm of the Possible attractive forces, having power to fix their lineaments, and shape living things, out of these creatures of our slumbers. The Unknown has power over these strange visions, and out of them composes monsters. Orpheus, Homer, and Hesiod imagined only the Chimera: Providence has created this terrible creature of the sea.

Creation abounds in monstrous forms of life. The wherefore of this perplexes and affrights the religious thinker.

If terror were the object of its creation, nothing could be imagined more perfect than the devil-fish.

The whale has enormous bulk, the devil-fish is comparatively small; the jararaca makes a hissing noise, the devil-fish is mute; the rhinoceros has a horn, the devil-fish has none; the scorpion has a dart, the devil-fish has no dart; the shark has sharp fins, the devil-fish has no fins; the vespertilio-bat has wings with claws, the devil-fish has no wings; the porcupine has his spines, the devil-fish has no spines; the sword-fish has his sword, the devil-fish has none; the torpedo has its electric spark, the devil-fish has none; the toad has its poison, the devil-fish has none; the viper has its venom, the devil-fish has no venom; the lion has its talons, the devil-fish has no talons; the griffon has its beak, the devil-fish has no beak; the crocodile has its jaws, the devil-fish has no teeth.

The devil-fish has no muscular organisation, no menacing cry, no breastplate, no horn, no dart, no claw, no tail with which to hold or bruise; no cutting fins, or wings with nails, no prickles, no sword, no electric discharge, no poison, no talons, no beak, no teeth. Yet he is of all creatures the most formidably armed.

What, then, is the devil-fish? It is the octopus, the sea vampire.

The swimmer who, attracted by the beauty of the spot, ventures among breakers in the open sea, where the still waters hide the splendours of the deep, or in the hollows of unfrequented rocks, in unknown caverns abounding in sea plants, testacea, and crustacea, under the deep portals of the ocean, runs the risk of meeting it. If that fate should be yours, be not curious, but fly. The intruder enters there dazzled; but quits the spot in terror.

This frightful apparition, which is always possible among the rocks in the open sea, is a greyish form which undulates in the water. It is of the thickness of a man's arm, and in length nearly five feet. Its outline is ragged. Its form resembles an umbrella closed, and without handle. This irregular mass advances slowly towards you. Suddenly it opens, and eight radii issue abruptly from around a face with two eyes. These radii are alive: their undulation is like lambent flames; they resemble, when opened, the spokes of a wheel, of four or five feet in diameter. A terrible expansion! It springs upon its prey.

The devil-fish harpoons its victim.

It winds around the sufferer, covering and entangling him in its long folds. Underneath it is yellow; above, a dull, earthy hue: nothing could render that inexplicable shade dust coloured. Its form is spider-like, but its tints are like those of the chamelion. When irritated it becomes violet. Its most horrible characteristic is its softness.

Its folds strangle, its contact paralyses.

It has an aspect like gangrened or scabrous flesh. It is a monstrous embodiment of disease.

It adheres closely to its prey, and cannot be torn

away; a fact which is due to its power of exhausting air. The eight antennae, large at their roots, diminish gradually, and end in needle-like points. Underneath each of these feelers range two rows of pustules, decreasing in size, the largest ones near the head, the smaller at the extremities. Each row contains twenty-five of these. There are, therefore, fifty pustules to each feeler, and the creature possesses in the whole four hundred. These pustules are capable of acting like cupping-glasses. They are cartilaginous substances, cylindrical, horny, and livid. Upon the large species they diminish gradually from the diameter of a five-franc piece to the size of a split pea. These small tubes can be thrust out and withdrawn by the animal at will. They are capable of piercing to a depth of more than an inch.

This sucking apparatus has all the regularity and delicacy of a key-board. It stands forth at one moment and disappears the next. The most perfect sensitiveness cannot equal the contractibility of these suckers; always proportioned to the internal movement of the animal, and its exterior circumstances. The monster is endowed with the qualities of the sensitive plant.

This animal is the same as those which mariners call Poulps; which science designates Cephalopterae, and which ancient legends call Krakens. It is the English sailors who call them 'Devil-fish,' and sometimes Bloodsuckers. In the Channel Islands they are called *pieuvres*.

They are rare at Guernsey, very small at Jersey; but near the island of Sark are numerous as well as very large.

An engraving in Sonnini's edition of Buffon represents a Cephaloptera crushing a frigate. Denis Montfort, in fact, considers the Poulp, or Octopod, of high latitudes, strong enough to destroy a ship. Bory Saint Vincent doubts this; but he shows that in our regions they will attack men. Near Brecq-Hou, in Sark, they show a cave where a devil-fish a few years since seized and drowned a lobster-fisher. Peron and Lamarck are in error in their belief that the 'poulp' having no fins cannot swim. He who writes these lines has seen with his own eyes, at Sark, in the cavern called the Boutiques, a pieuvre swimming and pursuing a bather. When captured and killed, this specimen was found to be four English feet broad, and it was possible to count its four hundred suckers. The monster thrust them out convulsively in the agony of death.

When swimming, the devil-fish rests, so to speak, in its sheath. It swims with all its parts drawn close. It may be likened to a sleeve sewn up with a closed fist within. The protuberance, which is the head, pushes the water aside and advances with a vague undulatory movement. Its two eyes, though large, are indistinct, being of the colour of the water.

When in ambush, or seeking its prey, it retires into itself, grows smaller and condenses itself. It is then scarcely distinguishable in the submarine twilight.

At such times, it looks like a mere ripple in the water. It resembles anything except a living creature.

The devil-fish is crafty. When its victim is unsuspicious, it opens suddenly.

A glutinous mass, endowed with a malignant will, what can be more horrible?

It is in the most beautiful azure depths of the limpid water that this hideous, voracious polyp delights. It always conceals itself, a fact which increases its terrible associations. When they are seen, it is almost invariably after they have been captured.

At night, however, and particularly in the hot season, it becomes phosphorescent. These horrible creatures have their passions; their submarine nuptials. Then it adorns itself, burns and illumines; and from the height of some rock, it may be seen in the deep obscurity of the waves below, expanding with a pale irradiation—a spectral sun.

The devil-fish not only swims, it walks. It is partly fish, partly reptile. It crawls upon the bed of the sea. At these times, it makes use of its eight feelers, and creeps along in the fashion of a species of swift-moving caterpillar.

It has no blood, no bones, no flesh. It is soft and flabby; a skin with nothing inside. Its eight tentacles may be turned inside out like the fingers of a glove.

It has a single orifice in the centre of its radii, which appears at first to be neither the vent nor the mouth. It is, in fact, both one and the other. The orifice performs a double function. The entire creature is cold.

The jelly-fish of the Mediterranean is repulsive. Contact with that animated gelatinous substance which envelopes the bather, in which the hands sink, and the nails scratch ineffectively; which can be torn without killing it, and which can be plucked off without entirely removing it—that fluid and yet tenacious creature which slips through the fingers, is disgusting; but no horror can equal the sudden apparition of the devil-fish, that Medusa with its eight serpents.

No grasp is like the sudden strain of the cephaloptera.

It is with the sucking apparatus that it attacks. The victim is oppressed by a vacuum drawing at numberless points: it is not a clawing or a biting, but an indescribable scarification. A tearing of the flesh is terrible, but less terrible than a sucking of the blood. Claws are harmless compared with the horrible action of these natural air-cups. The talons of the wild beast enter into your flesh; but with the cephaloptera it is you who enter into the creature. The muscles swell, the fibres of the body are contorted, the skin cracks under the loath-some oppression, the blood spurts out and mingles horribly with the lymph of the monster, which clings to its victim by innumerable hideous mouths. The hydra incorporates itself with the man; the man becomes one with the hydra. The spectre lies upon you: the tiger can only devour you; the devil-fish, horrible, sucks your life-blood away. He draws you to him, and into himself; while bound down, glued to the ground, powerless, you feel yourself gradually emptied into this horrible pouch, which is the monster itself.

Such was the creature in whose power Gilliatt had fallen for some minutes.

The monster was the inhabitant of the grotto; the terrible genii of the place. A kind of sombre demon of the water.

All the splendours of the cavern existed for it alone.

On the day of the previous month when Gilliatt had first penetrated into the grotto, the dark outline, vaguely perceived by him in the ripples of the secret waters, was this monster. It was here in its home.

When entering for the second time into the cavern in pursuit of the crab, he had observed the crevice in which he supposed that the crab had taken refuge, the pieuvre was there lying in wait for prey.

Is it possible to imagine that secret ambush?

No bird would brood, no egg would burst to life, no flower would dare to open, no breast to give milk, no heart to love, no spirit to soar, under the influence of that appari-tion of evil watching with sinister patience in the dusk.

Gilliatt had thrust his arm deep into the opening; the monster had snapped at it. It held him fast, as the spider holds the fly.

He was in the water up to his belt; his naked feet clutching the slippery roundness of the huge stones at the bottom; his right arm bound and rendered powerless by the flat coils of the long tentacles of the creature, and his body almost hidden under the folds and cross folds of this horrible bandage.

Of the eight arms of the devil-fish three adhered to the rock, while five encircled Gilliatt. In this way, clinging to the granite on the one hand, and with the other to its human prey, it enchained him to the rock. Two hundred and fifty suckers were upon him; tormenting him with agony and loathing. He was grasped by gigantic hands, the fingers of which were each nearly a yard long, and furnished inside with living blisters eating into the flesh.

As we have said, it is impossible to tear oneself from the folds of the devil-fish. The attempt ends only in a firmer grasp. The monster clings with more determined force. Its effort increases with that of its victim; every struggle produces a tightening of its ligatures.

Gilliatt had but one resource, his knife.

His left hand only was free; but the reader knows with what power he could use it. It might have been said that he had two right hands.

His open knife was in his hand.

The antenna of the devil-fish cannot be cut; it is a leathery substance impossible to divide with the knife, it slips under the edge; its position in attack also is such that to cut it would be to wound the victim's own flesh.

The creature is formidable, but there is a way of resisting it. The fishermen of Sark know this, as does any one who has seen them execute certain movements in the sea. The porpoises know it also; they have a way of biting the cuttle-fish which decapitates it. Hence the frequent sight on the sea of pen-fish, poulps, and cuttle-fish without heads.

The cephaloptera, in fact, is only vulnerable through the head.

Gilliatt was not ignorant of this fact.

He had never seen a devil-fish of this size. His first encounter was with one of the larger species. Another would have been powerless with terror.

With the devil-fish, as with a furious bull, there is a certain moment in the conflict which must be seized. It is the instant when the bull lowers the neck; it is the instant when the devil-fish advances its head. The movement is rapid. He who loses that moment is des-troyed.

The things we have described occupied only a few moments. Gilliatt, however, felt the increasing power of its innumerable suckers.

The monster is cunning; it tries first to stupefy its prey. It seizes and then pauses awhile.

Gilliatt grasped his knife; the sucking increased.

He looked at the monster, which seemed to look at him.

Suddenly it loosened from the rock its sixth antenna, and darting it at him, seized him by the left arm.

At the same moment it advanced its head with a violent movement. In one second more its mouth would have fastened on his breast. Bleeding in the sides, and with his two arms entangled, he would have been a dead man.

But Gilliatt was watchful. He avoided the antenna, and at the moment when the monster darted forward to fasten on his breast, he struck it with the knife clenched in his left hand. There were two convulsions in opposite directions; that of the devil-fish and that of its prey. The movement was rapid as a double flash of lightnings.

He had plunged the blade of his knife into the flat slimy substance, and by a rapid movement, like the flourish of a whip in the air, describing a circle round the two eyes, he wrenched the head off as a man would draw a tooth.

The struggle was ended. The folds relaxed. The monster dropped away, like the slow detaching of bands. The four hundred suckers, deprived of their sustaining power, dropped at once from the man and the rock. The mass sank to the bottom of the water.

Breathless with the struggle, Gilliatt could perceive upon the stones at his feet two shapeless, slimy heaps, the head on one side, the remainder of the monster on the other.

Fearing, nevertheless, some convulsive return of his agony, he recoiled to avoid the reach of the dreaded tentacles.

But the monster was quite dead.

Gilliatt closed his knife.

It was time that he killed the devil-fish. He was almost suffocated. His right arm and his chest were purple. Numberless little swellings were distinguishable upon them; the blood flowed from them here and there. The remedy for these wounds is sea-water. Gilliatt plunged into it, rubbing himself at the same time with the palms of his hands. The swellings disappeared under the friction.

By stepping further into the waters he had, without perceiving, approached to the species of recess already observed by him near the crevice where he had been attacked by the devil-fish.

This recess stretched obliquely under the great walls of the cavern, and was dry. The large pebbles which had become heaped up there had raised the bottom

the level of ordinary tides. The entrance was a
large elliptical arch; a man could enter by
stooping. The green light of the submarine grotto
penetrated into it and lighted it feebly.

It happened that, while hastily rubbing his skin,
Gilliatt raised his eyes mechanically.

He was able to see far into the cavern.

THE KRAKEN

Alfred Lord Tennyson

Below the thunders of the upper deep;
Far, far beneath in the abysmal sea,
His ancient, dreamless, uninvaded sleep
The Kraken sleepeth: faintest sunlights flee
About his shadowy sides: above him swell
Huge sponges of millennial growth and height;
And far away into the sickly light,
From many a wondrous grot and secret cell
Unnumber'd and enormous polypi
Winnow with giant arms the slumbering green.
There hath he lain for ages and will lie
Battening upon huge seaworms in his sleep,
Until the latter fire shall heat the deep;
Then once by man and angels to be seen,
In roaring he shall rise and on the surface die.

STAY
ON

TARGET

Here are details of other exciting TARGET titles. If you cannot obtain these books from your local bookshop, or newsagent, write to the address below listing the titles you would like and enclosing cheque or postal order— *not* currency—including 5p per book to cover postage and packing. Postage is free for orders in excess of three titles.

TARGET BOOKS,
Universal-Tandem Publishing Co.,
14 Gloucester Road,
London SW7 4RD

THE STORY OF THE LOCH NESS MONSTER 25p
Tim Dinsdale

0 426 10073 5   **A Target Mystery**

What mysterious entity lurks beneath the 1000 ft. deep, sinister-looking waters of Loch Ness in the Highlands of Scotland? Since the 1930s, men have sought the answer to this question. The author, a full-time, professional monster-hunter, tells you the history of the search for "Nessie", and her cousin "Morag", the monster of Loch Morar, and of the latest discoveries made with scientific equipment. *Fully illustrated with maps, photographs, and drawings.*

If you enjoyed this book and would like to have information sent you about other TARGET titles, write to the address below.

You will also receive:

A FREE TARGET BADGE!

Based on the TARGET BOOKS symbol—see front cover of this book—this attractive three-colour badge, pinned to your blazer-lapel, or jumper, will excite the interest and comment of all your friends!

and you will be further entitled to:

FREE ENTRY INTO THE TARGET DRAW!

All you have to do is cut off the coupon beneath, write on it your name and address *in block capitals*, and pin it to your letter. You will be advised of your lucky draw number. Twice a year, in June and December, numbers will be drawn 'from the hat' and the winner will receive a complete year's set of TARGET books.

Write to: TARGET BOOKS,
Universal-Tandem Publishing Co.,
14 Gloucester Road,
London SW7 4RD

———————————— cut here ————————————

Full name...

Address..

....

...............................County....................................

Age...............................